Society Against Nature:
The Emergence of Human Societies

Serge Moscovici

Translated by Sacha Rabinovitch

Humanities Press
1976

Published in the U.S.A. 1976 by
Humanities Press Inc.
Atlantic Highlands
New Jersey, N.J. 07716

Society Against Nature
This edition first published in 1976
by The Harvester Press Limited

This translation and arrangement
copyright © The Harvester Press Limited 1976

First published in France as
La société contre nature
copyright © Union Générale d'Editions 1972

Library of Congress Cataloging in Publication Data

Moscovici, Serge.
    Society against nature.

    Translation of La société contre nature.
    Includes bibliographical references.
        1. Social evolution   2. Society, Primitive.
    3. Man-Animal nature. I. Title.
    GN360.M6713 301.2 75-43527
    ISBN 0—391—00523—5

Computer typeset by Input Typesetting Ltd,
London
Printed in Great Britain by Redwood Burn Ltd,
Trowbridge, Wiltshire
Bound by Cedric Chivers Ltd, Portway, Bath

Contents

Introduction

1

Considering the failure of so many species to survive, the fact that man has done so is certainly to his credit. It confirms him in his belief that he belongs to a superior race, yet the problem of how he was first able to raise himself above all the other species – indeed above all the supposedly more primitive sub-divisions of his own species, such as savages or women – remains unsolved.

For a long time society seemed to be the answer to this problem. Man emerged from nature as a social being, and society is the negation of nature. Though this opposition was occasionally questioned – Hume, for instance, asserted that it was nothing else than a fiction[1] – the conviction that society is the prerogative of mankind and that it is an unnatural phenomenon predominated.

However we are now living in an age where established theories are continually being refuted rather than confirmed by scientific investigation. The idea that man is master and possessor of nature, that he dominates a material world of which he is wholly independent, seems less convincing now that we have become aware of the existence of animal societies and of problems such as those of curbing natural forces, population expansion, environmental resources and even scientific progress. We have come to wonder if man is not in fact part of this material world he manipulates. On the other hand individualism, together with the individualization of human actions, interests and relationships, tends to stress the contrast between nature and society. The individual is now the standard of reference in every sphere, be it physics, biology, economics or philosophy. Society on the contrary is an anti-natural and antagonistic association of miscellaneous purposes or independent molecules under constraint. Present-day social and political laws and institutions are the result and expression of such antagonisms.

Nonetheless socialization is also a characteristic of our age. In physics atoms move, are transformed and disintegrate in groups. In biology populations and not individuals determine the survival of a species. Animal societies are known to possess hierarchies and conventions. And as far as natural philosophy is concerned it is scientists as a community who work to discover the laws of the material world; just as cooperation replaces individual labour in material production, collective thought now tends to replace individual thought. Society as collectivity or statistical unit directly or indirectly influences our lives and the way in which we think. It has become the essence of reality, and might well come to represent the essence of mankind.

Thus the antithesis of nature and society has lost much of its relevance, and our social and political laws must be reformulated according to a new relationship. The data and the logic on which our theories of man's origins were based, as well as the opposition and antinomy of society and nature, should be revised in the light of new scientific discoveries and historical events.

2

What were the circumstances of man's departure from nature? What were the crucial factors in this break with the biological and material world? At a given stage in the process of humanization an anatomical and physiological transformation took place in a virtually stabilized organism. This sudden, all-or-nothing cortical transformation (comparable to the quantum jump of an electron to a higher orbit) provoked a rupture in the process of evolution. This 'crossing of the Rubicon' opened the way to speech, reasoning and tool-making. Man thence acquired the amazing flexibility and inventiveness which enable him to make use of most existing natural resources, to accumulate and transmit knowledge and thus to adapt with surprising ease to different natural environments. Most species require genetic mutations subject to hereditary delays before such adaptations can occur; in man the change is restricted to the skills he can acquire. Indeed Bergson asserted that a basic nature exists and acquired natures are superimposed upon it imitating, yet never merging with it. [2] Over the ages general determining factors have been replaced by specifically human determining factors, enabling man to create his own particular mode of existence in his natural environment. Man found himself in the unique situation of being able to dominate a world he could exploit at will.

Such, at least, is the generally accepted answer to our questions. And the inferences which may be drawn from it are valid so long as man's biological structure is seen as invariable and uninfluenced by his activities. However it is now common knowledge that man's organism and characteristics – his upright stance, brain volume, speech and so on – result from his ability to use the techniques and implements which hunting required. The genetic and social developments which distinguish him did not precede but followed these circumstances. Man is self-made in every respect. From the time he first became an autonomous entity his nature has always involved a degree of understanding and an ability to create, together with the control of purposeful gestures and appropriate implements. At no stage of his evolution has his nature been restricted to a purely organic or instinctive apparatus. This fact is confirmed by palaeontological interpretations of human biology which tend to lay more and more stress on human technology.

Similarly, although according to former theories the natural environment was little more than a geographical and geological dimension,[3] uniform, unvarying and unaffected by the creatures which inhabit and exploit it, research has revealed that each species has its own peculiar ecology, related to the surface distribution of the population and to the activities which induce it to exploit one resource rather than another. A forest may appear specific and uniform to the superficial observer; for each of the animal species inhabiting it it is a structured, diversified world of which only a fraction is familiar. Man's environment is peculiar not only in its multiplicity and dimensions – it covers the world – but it includes a man-produced flora and fauna in addition to and interacting with the other. The processes which have influenced and shaped the human biosphere make it specific.

The intrinsic and extrinsic factors which contributed to the emergence of man created a new set of relationships which directly involved specifically human activities and skills, for man's intervention in the environment has always been deliberate; in the process of creating his environment he became physiologically, psychologically and socially a man.

In my earlier work, *Essai sur l'histoire humaine de la nature,*[4] I maintained that the coexistence and succession of various, all equally natural environmental relations was possible. The relationship with which we are concerned here is that between man and the elements. My theory was based on a study of the human activities which produce previously unknown combinations of physical, chemical and genetic elements, and not simply artefacts. The terms natural and artificial do not necessarily imply on the one hand the organic nature of which we are part and on the other the inorganic nature we conquer and transform. Man's single-handed conflict with nature should be seen as a confrontation *within* nature; society is a crucial component of our vital constitution. Man participates *with* vegetation *against* animals, *with* electricity *against* mechanical power, in a continuous modification of the environment; the principles which unite him to his allies and oppose him to his enemies are precisely those which unite or oppose physical, biological and chemical beings. The bond between man and nature is also a bond between nature and nature. Man with his limbs, nerves and brain merges with the natural forces he pervades. Thus he *is* the horse, the force of gravity, electricity and vice versa. Centuries ago Antiphon declared that: 'Through our skills we acquire control over those things by which nature controls us.' Man and nature are not two independent entities. Man is neither distinct from matter nor imprisoned within it, spectator and actor with no alternative but to dominate. There is no clear distinction between what man has made of his environment and what exists independently. Tools and instruments were once seen as extensions of the human body. But automatic gadgets today are so completely self-governing and self-producing that they are more like independent living organisms; yet they are the product of human ingenuity. On the other hand physicists, chemists and mathematicians have discovered ways of producing physical or chemical 'species' that have no equivalent in 'nature', yet are essentially indistinguishable from species which have emerged independently of such experiments. In Mendeleyev's periodic table each element has its place, whether it was produced by nature or in a laboratory. It would be a misuse of language to call products of a laboratory 'artefacts' since they neither copy nor replace pre-existing natural structures. Laboratory 'species' might, furthermore, include our own, for our biological characteristics, our intellectual faculties, our organs and their functions are, as I have pointed out, products of our own activities.

Thus the relation is peculiar only in its modalities and, finally, in one of its terms; like all such relations it involves biology and ecology. The notion that nature is inhuman and man unnatural is totally invalid. No part of man is or ever was closer than any other to an ever-changing nature. What occurs once is continually recreated, only the modalities change. As Shakespeare said:

> over that art
> Which you say adds to nature, is an art
> That nature makes.[5]

Both arts merge to produce the human history of nature rather than the idealized natural history of man created by our imagination. The appearance of a crucial characteristic which marks the emergence of our species and its departure from all the others was not a break with nature. The elusive missing link between ape and man is a transition from an early, common history of which it was a product, to the specific history of man of which he is the agent. Since nothing was added which was not already there, the problem of the origins of our species become the problem of its adaptation to the material world.

Introduction

3

It is not so easy nowadays to believe that society is a human prerogative. In the past society was seen to oppose nature on three fronts, the technical, the genetic and the political. Man was a fragile, physically underprivileged being who, thanks to his exceptional gifts of intelligence and initiative, had succeeded in imposing his own technical world on a given, more or less static nature where other more robust species thrived. Thus human nature became divided; an artificial superstructure induced by circumstances was superimposed on the original nature. This was the inevitable consequence of culture and evolution.

One of the aims of society is to erect barriers against the individual instinctive urges which threaten collective organization. Such repression has both a negative and a positive aspect. On the one hand it is responsible for war, disease and madness; on the other for art, science, literature, myth and religion. If there is such a diversity of human social structures it is precisely because man's adaptation to environmental circumstances is not organic (or only minimally so) but technical. That which is common to all collectivities is natural, while their distinctive features are social. Man's primitive, original state is natural. Socially he is an individual involved in a system of distinct collective obligations. There have always been those who, like Bodin, Locke or Rousseau maintain that man in his primitive, natural state was a happier and a better creature than society has made him. But even they had to admit that if society was an evil, it was a necessary evil.

Claude Lévi-Strauss has added an anthropological dimension to the problem. According to him man is biologically as unselective and promiscuous as all other animals. The contrast between nature and culture is epitomized in the contrast between a promiscuous sexuality and a sexuality governed by regulations. According to Lévi-Strauss the prohibition of incest is the process through which nature overcomes itself, the spark that sets in motion a different more complex mechanism which controls, and simultaneously includes, more simple psychological mechanisms, just as these control and include simpler animal mechanisms. It creates and represents a new order.[6] Though this order has positive connotations it also implies female subordination, for it excludes women from active social participation.

There are certain parallels between such a theory and those of Rousseau and his forerunners. For these society created stability, differentiation and purposefulness. For Lévi-Strauss matrimonial laws regulate the division of property and power on a sexual basis: women are the currency serving to procure material advantages. Marriage would thus be the earliest manifestation of slavery, or of human beings serving as chattel for other human beings, two sections of humanity opposing and completing each other as nature and society mutually oppose and complete each other.

I have pointed out the similarity of these theories in order to show the immutability of certain concepts of reality according to which equality is natural and inequality social, since family, class and status could not exist without it. Social order represses natural chaos to ensure the stability which nature requires but has become incapable of maintaining. Society complements man's organic equipment, enabling him to dominate the natural world *and* his own nature. Society is thus essentially anti-natural.

However such notions presuppose a primitive biogenetic man whose existence science has failed to discover. Undoubtedly a biological organism is the first manifestation of all life. This is never improved or replaced; it evolves continually as a result of experience. The only 'natural' transition would be a man-animal or an animal-not-yet-man. But recent discoveries make the chances of finding this missing link ever more remote. *Homo sapiens, Homo erectus, Australopithecus,* and so on all include both a biological and a cultural component. Man emerged many times over and each species represents an evolution rather than a birth – a joint transformation of nature and society rather than a victory of the latter over the former.

On the other hand if we examine the permanent, mutually profitable associations formed by various animal species, the correlation between the demands of a particular environment and an organized, eminently social behaviour become apparent, as well as the fact that society exists wherever a relatively organized living substance is to be found. Moreover such an examination reveals the ability of non-human creatures to perform activities hitherto considered exclusively human, such as learning and inventing. Primates, dolphins and even birds are able to adopt and improve different behaviours. Their survival and reproduction depend largely on this ability, and their young are no more capable than human children of developing normally when they are deprived of maternal and congeneric contacts. Even at the lowest level of the evolutionary scale a totally biological, non-social being has not been found, while among the more developed animal species heirarchical and behavioural rules are transmitted from one generation to another through individual and social initiation. The social and the sexual reproduction of a population are more or less coextensive. Furthermore a significant phenomenon, to which I shall return later, is the variety of primate social structures within a given species, which suggests the possibility of a certain amount of independence from genetic determination.

Although man has been more successful then most species in finding an adequate form of society, the system as such is not unique, but corresponds to a tendency which is common to all living creatures. Most species exert some kind of control over the growth of groups and the transmission of specific characteristics: they try to maintain a balance between population and resources. Society is not an extrasomatic extension; it is a necessity. By controlling individual relationships it promotes adaptation, the reproduction of groups and the exploitation of resources, and thus influences the environment. Whereas society has been seen as depending on the environment, the dependence is in fact mutual. Nature and society are compatible and complementary. Society is 'a fundamental biological option comparable to bilateral symmetry rather than to the specialization of prehensile forelimbs'.[7] The consequences of this are significant. Man's emergence has been seen as something sensational which extracted him from nature to enclose him in society. But once we have realized that society was not born with us and can be found at every level of existence the theory becomes scientifically untenable.

African, American and Australian savages have practically vanished from the face of the earth. Societies which had stagnated for centuries are making up for lost time. In our view of humanity these populations formerly represented the natural state; their existence was primitive and unhistorical. They lacked the forms of government and property which would have made them the equals of their discoverers; their members did not reason according to the rules of logic and philosophy. Their moral institutions could not be judged by Judaeo-Christian standards and were thus abnormal. Dominated as they were by savage instincts their social systems could hardly be called societies. Anthropologists believed they had discovered the primeval animal or infantile form of existence from which our Western societies had evolved.

Our innate intolerance of otherness has led us to see nothing but a void where we ourselves are not mirrored and to qualify what is different as defective. This stems from the assumption that aboriginal societies are rudimentary forms of our own social systems, whereas they have simply evolved differently and perhaps resisted better than us the effects of time. Because of this intolerance our civilization has been more destructive than constructive.

Most nations are now independent and tend towards a common system of exchange. Those who were thought of as primitive have retired from the stage. We know today that the opposite of our society is really a different society, and that man is a different kind of primate, not simply a biological primate to which has been added something entirely new. The differences between human populations, like those between men and other species, are social, but they are also genetic. The division between artificial and natural is not clear-cut and positive; social behaviour is natural to all animals. Contemporary historical discoveries have revealed the fragility of such divisions and also how typical they are of Western culture.

On the other hand uncertainties still persist and time alone will put an end to controversy, even though traditional concepts are gradually losing ground as former opinions are continually revised. Thus when issuing in book form his article on the 'Super-Organic',[8] published forty years earlier, Alfred Kroeber questioned the validity of distinctions between the social and the organic, together with the theories on which such distinctions were based. Similarly Lévi-Strauss, when a new edition of *The Elementary Structures of Kinship*[9] appeared after twenty years, noted that nature and society could not readily be separated. He added that the opposition between the two terms is probably not inherent in the structure of reality, but an 'artificial' construct of the mind.

No one would suggest that these two eminent scholars could have based their earlier conclusions on insufficient data or faulty deductions. So perhaps the premises of these conclusions have been called in question by the present state of our knowledge. We are now aware that purely biological individuals and communities did not become social suddenly and spontaneously; they already possessed an organized form of social existence, a different kind of order which only seems disorderly because it is different. The society we call human did not start with man or vice-versa. We can safely assert that the first hominids possessed a social system more or less similar to that of the higher primates of today, and that this is what enabled them to survive and to evolve. Our society emerged from another society. And the present inquiry deals not with the social progress of a humanity suddenly erupting from nature, but with the human progress of society.

4

Nature and society are not mutually exclusive. Man is part of nature and he has contributed to its configuration. Society is a general phenomenon common to all species. Man is biological because he is social and social because he is biological, a specific product of neither nature nor society. If we cease to oppose society to nature the dividing line moves from the horizontal to the vertical plane dividing each internally instead of one from the other. Events, actions and phenomena will then assume a different relationship, and the elusive transition from nature to society will emerge as a parallel joint transition from a universal to a specifically human natural state, and from a general to a particular social structure. The object of this book is precisely to discover what provoked this transition; the outlook I advocate should make the task easier.

The transition from a passive to an active relationship with the environment was the result of:

firstly, a natural division of men according to resources and skills which replaced natural selection and assumed its function;

secondly, the mobility of populations and the development of aptitudes which replaced the adaptative modifications required by a given environment.

These substitutions led to the diversification of specific human physical-anatomical characteristics from those of anthropoids, a diversification which is generally attributed to genetic mutations or to a sudden dramatic change in the natural environment, that is to say to a precise organic or environmental cause. I see it as resulting from the development of latent anthropoid predacious and tool-making instincts in response to tensions in the social structure. The observation of somewhat similar phenomena in anthropoid societies has recently given rise to a great deal of literature in which approximate parallels between animal and human social behaviour are used to illustrate the identity of social and biological processes. The relations between sexes, generations and societies, social contracts, hunting, war and marriage are seen as the consequences of natural selection which is made to explain everything that occurs wherever human beings exist. However when such phenomena are considered objectively, they shatter our conception of biology and stress the significance of social dynamism in relation to the environment by exposing more particularly the specific character of humanization. The main point is not that our species should be descended from primates, but that we evolved from a population of gatherers; that from such a population emerged a society of hunters with their specific methods of dealing with the material world. In this light the limitations of natural selection become apparent, as well as the significance of what I have set in its place.

On the other hand human society replaced or remodelled primate societies by modifying the relation between generations and sexes. The institution of paternity and the family unit transformed the relationship between adult and young males; the prohibition of incest fixed the respective social positions of males and females, dividing them into distinct groups with different responsibilities and activities. The purpose of the prohibition was not to abolish sexual promiscuity (which even among animals is rare or non-existent), but to connect the society in which man lives with the environment he has created for himself; it served a similar function to thought, language, tools and so on. Paternity, the family and the prohibition of incest are different aspects of the transition from primate societies of affiliation to human kinship societies.

The idea of nature as universal and society as specific becomes less convincing once the mutual interaction of society and nature has been perceived. What is surprising is that more attention has not been given to this and that nothing has been done to revise the traditional concept; in physics, when a new situation arises, as for instance in the case of the atom, existing theories are thoroughly re-examined. But I can only try to define these two basic spheres of reality and stress their respective significance. Society is not against nature; it is part of nature and eminently natural. In the course of this work I have somtimes had to refer to research and theories from different branches of learning, but since I am well aware that such references lose much of their value when taken out of context, I have done so as sparingly as possible. I cannot claim that the inferences I have drawn from primate evolution or from non-Western civilizations have more than a potential significance for evolution and for civilization in general; only that they throw light on the direct relationships my theory involves. This is inevitable when different disciplines are made to cooperate in solving a common problem. Experts would be ill advised to object to my methods since they, justifiably, do not hesitate to stray beyond the limits of their own province. Indeed it is regrettable that they tend too often to do so indiscriminately, mainly to gain the approval of an audience whose conventional notions they strengthen rather than undermine. That is perhaps why so many revolutionary enterprises in palaeontology, anthropology and ethnology have completely misfired.

I hope that at least some of the theories I have expounded will appear true and original. I have always given my reasons for adopting or discarding a point of view; there may well be other equally valid reasons. I am sure that my theories are not unassailable, and I have no objection to some healthy scepticism, so long as it is not provoked by the unfamiliarity and unconventionality of my contentions.

Part One

Evolution and History

[I]

Early Primates

1 Society as Adaptation

Natural selection makes the best possible use of a population's organic predispositions in relation to its specific environment by merging the inevitable order and accidental results of phenomena. It controls the communications of genetic information capable of adapting to a given environment. But it is more than a means of relating a specific living organism – or genetic population – and a particular natural category to its distribution in time and in space. The members of a species have a common basic heredity; but they are not identical nor part of an undifferentiated whole. They form a more or less organized collectivity, a combination of diverse, discrete elements and a system of relationships. Reproduction is their greatest common denominator. But it is not an uncontrolled phenomenon and the process of adaptation required for a population's survival depends as much on its size as on individual skills. The dimension of a species is related to the dimensions and resources of its environment; it cannot increase beyond a given limit without endangering the survival of its members and the structure of the community. The actual selection of survivors and their number – or the adjustment of a biological pattern and the 'rating' of its increase – are related operations. Differential reproduction favouring one genotype at the expense of another is counterbalanced by discriminatory reproduction controlling individual procreation within the favoured genotype. It operates either by regulating the number of offspring each couple can produce, or by establishing a ratio between the number of adults involved in the reproducing cycle and the number excluded from it.

Thus Malthusianism is a permanent reality among animal populations living within the limits of a given environment and conditioned by a genetic structure. According to an appealing hypothesis,[1] confirmed by successive observations at various levels of the biological scale, a number of behavioural social phenomena such as display or aggression are directed towards the control of mating, birth and death ratios within a given species. Ritual or seasonal restrictions of sexual intercourse, reserved territories, hierarchies prescribing the availability of resources and sexual partners and the competitive attitudes consistent with a given optimum density are the processes that operate in the animal world to obtain a specific total of procreation potential, to distinguish the indispensable from the supernumerary members of a community and to compensate for a loss of 'manpower' due to excessive mortality.

Animal relationships are never haphazard. This applies to sexual relationships as well as to feeding and grooming priorities. Thus the network of collective relations influences the distribution of genetic material. The communal value of particular behaviour patterns overrules their individual value; the working order of the social mechanism depends on them and the survival of the community takes precedence over that of one of its members. A striking example of this peculiarity is the territorial behaviour of the male bird: his publicized presence makes him an easy prey, while its object is the partition of breeding territories to ensure the sustenance of the fledgelings; moreover by attracting predators to himself he averts them from the hen bird and her nestlings.

In most animal species social structure and selective process cooperate, since adaptation affects individuals through the collectivity. [2] Paradoxically enough the Mendelian revolution, which induced biologists to think in terms of populations rather than individuals, has simultaneously stressed both physico-chemical inter-nuclear dynamics and collective trans-individual dynamics, while the individual is increasingly seen as product rather than as the centre from which everything radiates and where all significant changes occur.

The study of animal societies and of why and how they operate is still in its infancy. It is based on conjecture rather than on experiment, and the point of view just mentioned owes as much to ignorance as to fact; further research is as likely to disprove as to confirm it. In the meantime we can infer that the relative importance of factors which influence the behaviour of a species and its reproduction – the pre-eminently directional mechanism – varies with the degree of evolution achieved. By and large biogenetic components exert a greater influence than biosocial among animal species. Since the environment is crucial, extinction or speciation (the reproductive isolation of a population which restricts the circulation of genetic information) are the direct consequences of overpopulation or of variations in individual adaptability to a given territory. Genetically favourable or unfavourable factors have immediate repercussions on the network of relations linking the members of a collectivity. A biological species is able to organize one, and only one, social system; nor does it require any other.

In evolution the genetic substratum is a necessary factor, environment a sufficient factor and society an incidental factor. Simians break with this rule. Ethologists soon became aware of the fact once they ceased to base their studies of animal behaviour on captive animals and began to observe wild beasts in their natural habitat. Instead of seeing them in relation to mankind as comparatively underdeveloped organisms, they appreciated them as creatures highly attuned to the requirements of their environment and worthy of being considered in their own right.

The advancement of learning invariably depends on the degree of respect accorded to the object of study, be it animal, vegetable or mineral, and on the scholar's self-effacement. It is not surprising that this new attitude has proved extremely fruitful. We now know that some primate communities are composed of a basic group including as a rule females, adolescents of both sexes and at least one adult male. Communal and procreative activities occur within this group, which is relatively stable and coherent. More or less freely dependent on such a group are a number of subsidiary groups of young adult males. The whole constitutes a society.

Let us examine two main examples of such societies. First the clan. Kummer and Kurt have called it a 'one male society'. This is misleading since it refers to sexual and not status distinctions, and since the dominant male is in fact frequently accompanied by a rightful claimant who follows or even replaces him in the mating hierarchy. However in such societies the basic group is, in effect, composed of an adult male and a number of females with their infant and adolescent offspring. Relations between basic group and sub-groups vary. Among geladas they congregate sporadically in order to exploit a richly productive territory. Among hamadryas — a type of large cynocephalic monkey noted for its mane and worshipped by the ancient Egyptians — the groups intermingle frequently and their relationship is relatively organized. In neither case are their territories strictly divided. Monosexual satellite groups of sub-adult males usually gravitate on the fringe of such groups. Within the basic group strict hierarchical behaviour is observed; the dominant male and master of ceremonies closely supervises his females and quells insubordination indiscriminately whether the culprit is an adolescent or an adult. Young males adopt a submissive attitude in his presence to placate him or win his favours. But the dominant male is not a chief, and in normal circumstances the females, who are alone responsible for their offspring, settle their own disputes. His role is rather that of a guardian in charge of the regular organization of his little tribe. With his superior experience, strength and authority he is invaluable in emergencies or during migrations. The punishments and privileges he metes out stress his inclusive or exclusive relationship to other members of the group. The basic group appears to be self-inclusive (in this sense it is a clan) and highly interdependent; as such it associates with the sub-groups.

Another type of society is the fraternity. Here members congregate more or less regularly to share a common activity; the barriers between groups are not hard and fast and males are seen to circulate from one to another. The society as a whole lives at the forest edge, on open ground or marshland, and roams relatively far afield and according to a well-defined routine. Some species defend their territory, but encroachments are tolerated. Fighting sometimes breaks out in frontier zones, but as a rule such confrontations are avoided and fraternities tend to ignore each other. There are sòcial sub-structures within each society involving, for instance, temporary regroupings at sleeping and feeding sites. These sub-structures are not self-contained and individuals pass from one to another according to circumstances.

Observations of macaque monkeys and baboons in the marshlands or wooded regions of Africa and Asia show that their daily activities follow a regular pattern and that members of a group are extremely interdependent; they never go singly to a drinking place and always move about in groups, mainly because of the danger presented by predators. Social coherence is maintained by a complex male hierarchy determining sexual and feeding priorities in which dominating members are privileged. When baboon and rhesus monkey females first come into rut they are usually mated by young, subordinate males, but later, at the climax, they copulate with higher-ranking animals. Such promiscuity is socially sanctioned. The group of dominating males controls the whole community, directs its activities and determines the status of each member.

2 *The Art of Survival*

These are two extreme types of primate society, but there are a number of intermediary forms.[3] Such diversity is not significant in itself but only in its intra-specific character: social structures vary within a given species, a fact which is confirmed by numerous observations of macaques and baboons.

What then predetermines primate collective existence? What are the reasons for this diversity of structures within a species and between species? And what is the evolutionary significance of such differences?

The traditional answer to the first question (whether it refers to primates or other species) is the sexual instinct. This answer is based on observations of the behaviour of animals in captivity, that is of animals outside their natural habitat and freed from the compulsion to fend for themselves. There is, moreover, a tendency to stress a reproductive urge underlying sexual intercourse and thus ultimately predetermining primate sociability.

Contemporary studies of wild animals in their natural surroundings have set sexual behaviour in a wider context where it acquires a less prominent position in the behavioural picture. But apart from this, the whole concept needs revising. Indeed, if animal social existence springs from the need to satisfy instinctive and mainly sexual needs, we must infer: firstly, that interactions with the environment are secondary and depend exclusively on genetic factors; secondly, that social relations are conditioned by procreativeness, that is by the ability to respond to instinctual demands; and thirdly, that reproduction is not a process but an activity, that is to say that it mediates individual relationships within the group but not the adaptation of the group with its environment. In fact the inference is that society is sexual, not sexuality social.

Such an explanation was acceptable so long as we judged animal behaviour by human standards and saw animal societies as extra-evolutionary, ignoring the general mechanisms which regulate population expansion or seeing them as merely accidental; and so long as we were unaware of intra-specific social variations. But the accumulation of observations and our increasing knowledge of society's role in evolution have made it obsolete.

Empirical evidence may not be entirely conclusive, but it does enable us to see the connection between primate societies and their habitat. John Crook and Stephen Gartlan (in a theoretical work which is quite remarkable in its approach even though it requires some amendments) divide primate social systems into five categories, ranging from the clan to the fraternity. Drawing up a table of correspondences between group size, type of basic organization, organization of daily activities, alimentary preferences, population distribution and the biotic characteristics of habitats, they connect the five categories respectively with forests, forest borders, marshland and variously arid territories. Adaptability is revealed in the similarity of social systems adopted by primates of different species living in similar environments, or in the parallel between system and environment. Social heterogeneity does not depend on the animals' genetic or instinctive equipment but on a population-habitat relation. For wherever selective pressure is operative, survival depends on the reproduction of the group and not on individual procreation.

On this basis it is possible to formulate a number of hypotheses — debatable, perhaps, but then we are breaking new ground — concerning the correspondence between social structure and environment. The clan is found mainly in arid regions where the threat from predators is relatively remote and food is scarce. Here the population is less dense than in more fertile territories — a fact which evidence confirms and which is, moreover, predictable since such environments would hardly encourage immoderate expansion; the ability of a population to reproduce itself would be decreased if it were too large in relation to available resources. The presence in such groups of a single adult male is self-explanatory: one male can impregnate a number of females, and when supplies are scarce, breeding must be reduced to a minimum if everyone is to be fed; indeed, only those societies survive where expansion does not exceed an optimum and where a balance has been achieved between the number of male and female animals. The clan maintains this balance by excluding the young males who congregate in a monosexual, satellite group on the fringe of the main group. Observations do not disprove such a hypothesis since the proportion of males to females reveals the expected disparity in hamadryas, geladas and patas communities living in unfertile regions.

Fraternities, on the other hand, live in marshlands and on the forest edge where climatic variations are less pronounced and food is more plentiful. Here the large dominant males with their smaller mates and offspring find sufficient nourishment, and communities, frequently consisting of hundreds of animals, roam considerable distances in quest of good feeding grounds; but competition between members or component groups is never sufficient to disrupt or otherwise impair the community. Discrimination between reproductive and non-reproductive males is also less marked and animals often switch from one group to another. The size of the community and the compulsory cooperation of its members constitute an effective protection against the numerous predators. According to a number of observations the animals are more skilful and possess a more complex system of vocal and facial communication than do species living in arid, sparsely wooded regions.

These accounts carry a lot of weight and their logic is compelling. Unfortunately, though they provide a list of correlations relative to the phenomena of social variability, they suggest no rigorous hypotheses about the causes and effects or the relation between them. Thus it is difficult to assert that they answer our question adequately. However what does emerge is that non-human primate social systems are determined at the level of the genotype. Each member has a specific function, a permanent programme of interchanges, a given sphere of experience to cope with and a living space of his own. His chances of breeding and so of surviving in his descendents depend on his ability to fit into the social framework. But this applies equally to the community as a whole. Compliance with social — and thus ecological — dictates is a condition of adaptation and the perpetuation of appropriate physical and anatomical characteristics. In order to survive a social structure has to control relations between members, preserve behavioural patterns which favour stability and maintain the frequency and character of social intercourse. Norms and patterns are transmitted from one generation to the next, imitated by contemporaries and imposed by senior on junior members. A group's preservation depends on its successful socialization, as does each member's chance of obtaining sufficient food and of advancing his position in the general hierarchy. The requirements of communal existence have the paradoxical effect of stressing individual dissimilarities at the level of the phenotype, that is of developing rather than eradicating personality. Sex, age and status comstitute a loose framework which does not strictly predetermine individual destinies.

Studies of primate communal existance based on detailed ethological reports show that a great variety of means, of behaviour, achieves similar ends. Ecological changes evidently create similarities in the social structure and relationships of neighbouring communities. But discrepancies in degrees of individual and communal freedom suggest that differences in basic social dynamics exert a powerful influence. Indeed it is legitimate to ask whether the environment really is such an important factor and whether these different types of society are invariably determined by external circumstances alone. For it is reasonable to presume that a community might sometimes seek a more suitable environment rather than adapt its requirements to the territory it inhabits. Thus the interplay of social and environmental adaptation might be responsible for the intermediary types of social structure observed among primates.

The relation between society and environment undoubtedly exists, but, as Ronald Hall has pointed out, it is very flexible. Rhesus monkeys and baboons survive equally well in forest or marshland; their organized, aggressive, versatile societies are precisely what one would expect of a species perfectly adapted to its environment. On the other hand the more peaceful entellus monkey inhabits similar and equally varied territories. Chimpanzees unquestionably control their forest habitat as efficiently as baboons and rhesus monkeys do theirs; yet their fraternities are loosely knit, unstable and relatively indifferent to territorial rights. Thus ecology predetermines the general structure of a society, but not its particular norms or behaviour; whence a certain amount of autonomy in social systems and their structure already among primates. Alterations in both the social and the material worlds have a concerted influence on the genetic sub-structure, that is on the species' adaptability and on its survival techniques. Though the range of such techniques is restricted, the choice is sufficiently wide to reduce the tendency to speciation (i.e. to reproductive isolation of populations) – though here the flexibility of their social structures plays an important part. With the multiplication of possible biological combinations the chances of survival increase and species are seen to thrive and breed in apparently dissimilar environments. Indeed through the dynamism and complexity of their ecology primates undergo widely varied forms and conditions of existence. In this way their biogenetic and biosocial potential is thoroughly exploited. We have seen that rhesus monkeys, baboons and chimpanzees survive in forest or marshland, dwelling in trees and bushes or on the ground; that variations in the size and density of a society, in the behaviour and relationships of its members and the division between reproductive and non-reproductive males successfully counteract speciation. Such versatility must have fostered adaptability, facilitating the task of supernumerary members who had to seek new environments where their means of existence rather than their genotype is modified. In this respect natural selection hs no further role to play. In primates direct pressure of ecological factors on genetic structure and on social relations are no longer the sole mechanism of evolution and are not alone responsible for adaptation. By a reversal of priorities the predominant traditions and associations which govern breeding, feeding, migrations and the division of labour *within* an animal community partially influence the extent and diversity of its relation to the environment. Thus the historical process is grafted onto the process of evolution.

[II]

Societies Without Speech

1 *Well-tempered Hierarchies*

Primates represent a turning-point in the development of relations with the material world. Man was at the same crossroads many centuries ago and has left it far behind him. In the hope of discovering what provoked this crisis, the preliminary conditions of which we have already outlined, I shall dwell a little longer on primate social structures because of the similarities which they offer with our own earliest societies. Indeed the mutual relationships and practical and symbolic behaviour of cynocephalus and anthropoid monkeys often strike us as differing from what we find in some human societies, even today, only in that the monkeys lack speech. However for such comparisons to be fruitful we should avoid the common tendency to see these animal communities as primitive examples of our own perfected structures, thus ignoring the originality of their systems and minimizing the fact that these are mature societies arrived at after a long evolutionary process. Their particularity does not reside in the biological identity of their members. (i.e. non-human primates), for it seems that the first hominids were similar in their manner of life. Nor is it very helpful to define a social system as human or animal, since both human and animal societies, past and present, are so varied in pattern. For the sake of clarity we shall describe the societies with which we are concerned as *societies of affiliation,* in view of a feature they all share.

The members of such societies constantly seek the reassurance of each other's company and support. Relationships are not mediated by specialized social bodies. Their overt behaviour clearly defines the respective status of members and of groups, the distribution of resources and the privileges of status. Roles are enforced by incitement and are clear, but flexible and interchangeable. Thus a hamadryas baboon may be a dominant male in one group, then switch to a satellite non-reproductive group, and eventually recover his former status. But at each stage of his existence an animal fulfils a given function with its specific code of behaviour in a consistent framework where he learns who may be safely approached and who avoided. Isolation is dangerous, for it deprives the individual of social protection and stimulus. Observation confirms that in all species socialization owes more to the need for affiliation than to ecological or territorial pressures.

Michael Chance and Clifford Jolly in their compelling book, *Social Groups of Monkeys, Apes and Men*,[4] describe the stem structure of affiliation societies and distinguish three typical sub-groups. The first is the *assembly of females* with or without progeny which is mainly conspicuous when the band is inactive, that is neither feeding nor evading attack. At such times the younger or childless members are allowed to look after the infants, groom them or play with them. Such assemblies are a distinctive feature of primate societies. Although their structure is relatively flexible compared to male sub-divisions, the avoidance of higher- by lower-ranking females indicates the presence of a hierarchy. This social feature is particularly pronounced in communities where the females enjoy a certain amount of freedom and it is partly or totally absent in species where intersexual relationships predominate; as in the case of rhesus monkeys, who occasionally form more or less permanent couples; or gibbons where such couplings are the norm. Hamadryas (who tend to congregate around a single male) and hooded macaques cannot properly be said to have assemblies of females.

Different age groups congregate in *adolescent gangs* for feeding expeditions and games. Older animals can frequently be seen carrying the younger, especially in critical situations such as the approach of a high-ranking animal or a threat of any kind. Among geladas or hamadryas the social flexibility of these gangs is such that they may even include youngsters from various single-male groups. In some communities adolescents are relegated to the periphery, while in others they are allowed to play among their seniors so long as they do not disturb them. However patas monkey adolescent gangs tend to merge with the assemblies of females, whereas young gorillas play among their elders or in independent gangs.

The adult males form a ranked *cohort* and rarely participate singly in any kind of activity. Among gorillas and macaques as well as among the heterosexual communities of baboons living in marshlands the cohort consists of reproductive males. As to the non-reproductive, or peripheral 'bachelors', all that can be ascertained to date is that even when they associate with reproductive males their group does not disband; little attention has been given to such groups which have generally been considered of minor interest. Another undeservedly neglected phenomenon is the apparently unmotivated disbanding of some cohorts (chimpanzee, for instance) and their regrouping in bisexual units. The degree of integration of male cohorts varies with the species. Among patas and entellus they do not associate with the main group formed by the dominant male and his females, whereas among geladas they associate but without actually merging; chimpanzee cohorts sometimes detach themselves from the main group for several days, while the gorilla cohort and heterosexual group are completely amalgamated.

The perusal of a city or village plan usually gives one a rough idea of the classes of people who inhabit it and of the way the different classes interrelate. And by studying the spatial distribution of a primate community one gets an equally clear idea of the individual and sub-group priorities which distinguish it. The activity of Japanese monkeys, for instance, is restricted by an ideal system of concentric circles in which animals occupy a predetermined place. In the centre or inner circle are the dominant male or 'coryphaeus' (an apter term than 'chief' or 'leader') with the adult females and (mainly female) infants; the next circle includes the 'second strings' and juvenile males; while the 'bachelor' adult males are relegated to the outer circle.

Such a layout is remarkably consistent. In Takasakiyama, where these observations were made, though the number of monkeys practically trebled in five years, the alpha-coryphaeus, or principal male, continued to occupy the same social and spatial position. The adult subordinate males and the adolescent males also maintained both status and spatial allocation. On the other hand two of the five dominant males and five of the eight juvenile males moved from their respective circles to the periphery where they joined the group of bachelor males. Some nursing females with their infants also emigrated to the outer circle where their movements were less restricted. But on the whole it would seem that the social barriers are both unscalable and efficient.

Similarly a group of baboons on the move – which may include from twelve to eighty-seven animals – is thoroughly organized, especially in open territory. At first glance the procession may seem uncoordinated, but in fact a number of subordinate males and a couple of adolescents invariably constitute the vanguard, followed by a few females and most of the adolescents; then come the coryphaeus males, the nursing females with their progeny and the pre-adolescent animals; in the rear, mirroring the vanguard, are females, adolescents and, lastly, subordinate males. In such spontaneously adopted formations it is clear that the females, infants and coryphaeus males occupy the most sheltered position, while the procession as a whole can be supervised from this vantage point by the animals responsible for its safe conduct and for making emergency decisions in moments of uncertainty or danger.

The organization of chimpanzee communities and migrations is looser and more complex; they are also less permanent and exclusive. Observations carried out in the Budoryo forests listed communities consisting of: (a) adult males only; (b) adult males and females with an occasional adolescent; (c) mothers with their progeny; and (d) mothers with their progeny, childless females, adolescents and adult males. Elsewhere troops including nothing but males were seen to split temporarily into sub-groups or to join up with adolescents and females. But not withstanding such apparent versatility and anarchy the male sub-group invariably dominates the rest of the community.

Remarkable as such spatial organization may be in all respects, what mainly emerges is its hierarchical character. This is a feature of all primate communities, though it operates in different ways and to different ends. Indeed because it assumes such varied forms and combines three dissimilar functions (control, dominance and influence) it is hard to define it with any precision.

Rank order controls social organization through the medium of male relationships with females and young. In all the species observed male animals always have precedence and, in relation to this, competition between the sexes has never been noted. Since their position is uncontested the males set the standard for female behaviour and status, controlling the whole system of female priorities and communication.

The specific channels through which communication travels in a primate community are reflected in the way innovations spread among its members. Some Japanese scholars noticed that a group of young monkeys on the island of Koshima had taken to washing sweet potatoes before eating them, after seeing an eighteen-month-old female do so. However none of the older males — who did not normally mix with the adolescents — followed suit. To test the hypothesis such behaviour suggested, the scholars offered some toffee to the young monkeys who gradually became extremely fond of this new delicacy; the taste for toffee later spread to the mothers and their infants, but never to the adult males. Yet when some corn was offered to the dominant male, he took it at once and was soon joined, first by the higher-ranking females and then by the other members of the community; and this in the space of a few hours, whereas it had taken eighteen months to persuade half the community to eat toffee. Thus hierarchy seems to play an important part in the inhibition and promotion of behaviour. Top-ranking animals set the example for the participation or non-participation of the community whose enforced dependence contributes to the stability of the group.

Though female geladas are allowed a certain amount of freedom they still congregate regularly around the dominant male, whether invited or not. They are constantly aware of his movements and at the slightest sign of restlessness on his part they instantly get ready to follow him. He too watches them all the time, checking the presence of each one; should he notice that a female is missing he takes a threatening attitude, head thrown back, tail held high, and scans the group searchingly. When a female misbehaves in one way or another he goes up to her; she immediately crouches down submissively and emits a piercing cry while looking up at him beseechingly till he sits down beside her and she starts to groom him.

The hamadryas female baboon follows the male everywhere, never straying more than a couple of yards from his side. She obeys him implicitly, and should she show any sign of waywardness he calls her to order by a sharp nip on the neck. His purpose is to maintain the unity of the community and enforce loyalty among all its members, but especially among the females. The amount of control he exerts is expressed in his attitude to females and to juveniles mainly of the female sex. A female's attitude to other females reflects her relation to the dominant male. Thus when a female has succeeded in securing a place of honour beside him she is emboldened to attack her rivals or chase them away. The male rarely intervenes in such quarrels, but when he does it is invariably to assist the female who is nearest to him.

Rank is associated more or less rigidly with control according to the species, but it invariably dictates the female's attitude in her dealings with males or with other females.

The hierarchy of dominance isolates and mutually opposes adult males as the privileged position of the coryphaeus is envied by his less fortunate contemporaries and by his juniors. For geladas and hamadryas, who live in clans, the problem is less acute since the underprivileged males are segregated in a monosexual, peripheral or satellite sub-group. Only rarely do they succeed in avoiding such a fate when they manage to become second-in-command to an aging coryphaeus. This consists in directing operations during expeditions; but the younger animal still has to report the general progress to his more experienced senior who makes all the important decisions.

Hierarchical distinctions are more obvious in baboon communities, where lower-ranking animals always make way for the higher when they meet and dominant males have first choice at sleeping sites. In these fraternities hegemony takes the form of a 'chieftainry' or association of dominant males. Status does not depend exclusively on physical aptitudes such as power or agility, but on a system of alliances as well. The dominant animals usually go out in groups to assist each other against attacks from predators or outsiders. Such a custom may well derive from the fact that they inhabit regions where beasts of prey are plentiful, but their multiple leadership certainly helps to maintain a relatively strict discipline in the community. Fights are rare; Japanese scholars observed only a small percentage of such outbreaks in the communities they were studying, and these were promptly quelled by the dominant males. A hierarchy of dominance is remarkably enduring, probably because it represents the authority of a sub-group of the population rather than that of a single animal.

Social distinctions based on influence are less readily discernible and usually restricted to adult and juvenile male relationships. The senior animals have to ensure their juniors' compliance with implicit social rules and respect for ranking orders. These adolescents – unlike the subordinate adult males – represent only a potential threat to the establishment. The mutual reactions of these two groups of animals have never been subjected to any serious study or observation; yet the presence of male juveniles undoubtedly constitutes a disturbing factor, for once a society has been created it tends towards permanence, opposing any attempt at innovation. An important male sub-group claiming its share of resources and social participation presents an unquestionable threat to such permanence, and in the absence of an adequate system of renewal the threat is all the greater.

At least one thing is certain: in most societies of affiliation the young females are retained within the basic group and enjoy very little freedom, whereas the young males are excluded and compelled to undergo an apprenticeship of independent survival. Such behaviour, as we have seen, has been observed among macaques, where the young males leave the inner circle and cease to mix with the rest of the community in which thereafter they play hardly any part.

The reader may be surprised that I should talk of a hierarchy of influence when what I refer to seems in fact to be a parent-child relationship. However it is always misleading to apply the categories of a society based on family ties to a society based on affiliation. Primate communities depend on the dominant adult male group's superiority and thus on the estrangement of the dominant males from the other male members and from their progeny as such. The father's relation to his male descendants is authoritarian; he seeks to minimize their initiative and reduce the danger of their interference in ordinary social activities. In such circumstances it is impossible to 'recognize a kinship between father and sons; this is not only true objectively, but the son has no awareness of having a "father" either.' [5]

Hierarchy in its different forms is not unmotivated; it has positive consequences for those it favours. The chances of survival for high-ranking animals are far greater, both individually and genetically, since they are better protected and have undisputed rights to nourishment and to heterosexual relationships. Subordinate animals, on the other hand, especially young adult or adolescent males, are banned from the community and have to lead a strictly monosexual life; their intercourse with females is difficult and hazardous, owing to the dominant male group's constant supervision, and lasting heterosexual relationships are practically impossible.

I should like to note in passing that although the theory concerning the feeding priorities of dominant males is plausible I have, as yet, come across no irrefutable proof of its truth. If it were confirmed we would have to infer that animals living on the social periphery – and especially monosexual groups – incur a much higher mortality rate than that recorded among top-ranking animals living in bisexual groups; but at present such an assertion is unwarranted. Grooming however, which is another status-defining process, has been unanimously confirmed. It consists in removing parasites and dirt from an animal's fur, and has obvious biological consequences. In regions where the majority of other wild animals are plagued with ticks, baboons, who spend a lot of their time grooming each other, are free from such parasites. Moreover, this hygienic activity, which indisputably contributes to the animals' well-being, creates subtle and complex relationships. In primate communities all the animals groom each other, but the amount of grooming each animal receives varies with his rank. Thus a high-ranking male is groomed more frequently than a lower-ranking animal; and by observing the pattern of any one animal's grooming habits — who grooms him and whom he grooms — it would be possible to tell who are his patrons and who his dependants.

We must bear in mind that hierarchies are not always as clearly defined as the above descriptions might lead one to suppose. They are extremely fluid among certain capucin monkeys, chimpanzees or entellus in India. Dominant males are frequently little more than guardians of the peace who separate litigants or signal the approach of danger. Neither is the interplay between the three hierarchical functions always constant, and they tend to be more coherently interdependent in clan societies than in fraternities.

2 The Demands of Social Life

Communal existence has no clearly defined rules. Nonetheless it obeys a system of tacit agreements which a member has to respect in order to remain within the group and maintain his status. The system has two main dimensions: sex and age. An individual's inclusion within one of these classes is less a matter of anatomy or physiology than of social convention. Females are required to be submissive, yet their status has a certain ambivalence, for they are not precisely subordinates and though part of the general hierarchical system they are somehow beyond its dominance and control. The female usually, but not invariably, acquires the status of her mate. The rank of an adult female rhesus monkey conditions the rank of her group in relation to neighbouring groups. The female baboon hierarchy, which is not clearly defined, is independent from that of the males. The female patas enjoy a strict hierarchy respected by the whole community, dominant male included; indeed if he happens to threaten a high-ranking female's progeny she immediately retaliates and is backed by all the other females.

The English ethologist Ronald Hall believes that though the dominant male is responsible for control, leadership and defence he is elected by the well-organized female group. Male and female groups appear to be relatively independent. Their division corresponds to a division of purpose. The male group is, on the whole, the less stable element of the community; the (adult) female group the more permanent. Observations on the development of a rhesus monkey community reveal that female groups are more homogeneous than male; they constitute the nucleus subsequently joined by the males to form the basis of a community.

If the permanence of social existence depends on the behaviour of female animals, the presence of the dominant male is nonetheless essential to the survival and coherence of the community. Animals who have not found a place within the system of relationships remain aloof or join a monosexual male gang. Among *Papio anubis,* vervets and in most fraternities the males pass from one sub-group to another with relative ease, whereas the female hierarchy is more consistent. The same phenomenon occurs among hamadryas baboons, where the dominant male keeps his females under strict supervision, never allowing any one of them to stray, while the sub-adult males can come and go at leisure so long as they respect the established priorities of the community.

But the inequality of the sexes spreads to every level of existence. Until their maturity the males are more or less compelled to congregate in satellite non-reproductive sub-groups. Thus they switch back and forth from a homosexual to a heterosexual social system, and each time they must learn to adapt to different, and even contradictory conventions and aims. This has far-reaching influences on their status and habits. In such conditions it is not surprising that some males choose to lead an anchoretic existence rather than undergo the stress of continuous change and the competitive tension of temporary heterosexual relationships.

The females, on the other hand, spend their whole lives within the basic heterosexual group. They may retire occasionally to the social periphery, but without ever actually abandoning the community, for this would not be tolerated by the dominent males. Yet it is the females who mediate between the two basic social units, the mother-son unit and the reproductive male-female unit, and thus constitute the pivot around which the community is organized.

These two units are distinct, since up to a certain age the young belong exclusively to the mother from whom they acquire their social status. A mother nurses her young for at least ten months, during which time she provides the emotional security they require and teaches them to explore their surroundings in search of food. In addition they learn from her example the social behaviour required by their particular status. Baboon and macaque mothers tend to be possessive with their young, while entellus mothers enrol other females to help look after their new-born infants.

The banishment of young males seems to be a general practice and they therefore become independent from their mothers sooner than their sisters. Yet the mother-son relationship, brief as it may be, does leave its mark. A penetrating study of rhesus monkeys at Cayo Santiago (Puerto Rico) reveals that the relationship is not entirely severed even after physical maturity. Preferential relationships also persist between siblings, who continue to groom each other as adults. Moreover juvenile males who try to join a peripheral monosexual gang are invariably rejected unless they can find an ally in the gang who, as far as one can judge, is a member of the youngster's clan.

The male member of the reproductive unit has only a casual relationship with his progeny. Research to date proves that 'paternal' behaviour is practically non-existent in affiliation societies, where dominant males are more possessive with the mothers than with their young. The Japanese scientist Itani noticed behaviour which could be called 'paternal' in only three communities out of the eighteen he observed. And adult male rhesus monkeys pay little attention to their offspring, when they are not positively hostile. However it should not be inferred that the community as a whole neglects the well-being and survival of the younger generation. As we have seen, childless animals of both sexes commonly assume the role of 'aunt' or 'uncle'. But it cannot be denied that adult males have a more lasting relationship with their female than with their male progeny who are banished from the inner circle at the approach of maturity.

This absence of a specific link between the males of two successive generations means that the permanence of the mother-son unit and that of the reproductive unit are mutually conflicting. The reproductive unit clearly defines the male's sphere of protection and dominance, his privileges and the restricted but regular pattern of his sexual activity. It emerges as an essential feature of the social system, partaking simultaneously of both male and female status and setting the boundaries between inner and peripheral circles.

The mother-son unit is less obvious and explicit because it is contained entirely within the female universe. It serves to create permanent mutual relationships stemming from a female or group of females. Thus it is neither transitory nor exclusively biological. It has been suggested that it can produce whole dynasties with connections spreading beyond the original community. Though it is impossible to verify conclusively such an hypothesis, it is logically feasible.

The transition from one unit to the other is ensured by the mother who is the affiliatory stem and the agent through whom a male's status is transmitted – though he is not aware of the fact. Observations of macaques have established that all adolescent males are banished to the social periphery – and so to a lower rank – except for the offspring of high-ranking females, who remain within the inner circle. They thus accede automatically to a status which normally requires a preliminary sojourn in 'purgatory' lasting from three to five years. Such a dispensation has obvious consequences and ensures the transmission of status priorities. The offspring of high-ranking females inevitably conform to the assertive aggressive attitude of their elders, while the young of subordinate females are submissive and timid. The former eventually dominate the latter since they have grown up within the dominant male's circle where the lower-ranking animals have always submitted to them and will naturally continue to do so.

Since the dominant group's welfare is an asset to the society as a whole, subordinate animals unquestioningly pamper and protect its members, thus ensuring their chances of survival. It follows that rank in such societies is not aleatory, intermittent or purely biological. For if the qualities required for the various responsibilities an animal must assume are predetermined by birth, a particular set of circumstances also ensures that the young will partake of their parents' social status. The link between the generations and the succession of status are provided by the mother, and the process itself ensures, with the transmission of status distinctions, the stability of the social structure.

The overall structure of societies of affiliation is based on some system of male hierarchy. If we examine the structure of the basic group (we saw above that it would be misleading to call it a 'family'), we find a fairly strict division of individual priorities and rules of conduct. Transgressions generally have painful consequences for the transgressor — sexual behaviour being no exception to this rule, though the problem has not been sufficiently investigated to reveal an exact mating code. On the evidence we possess it is legitimate to assume that the sexual behaviour of primates is not, broadly speaking, promiscuous. In clan societies particularly males sometimes mate exclusively with their own females in more or less regular rotation, according to age and sexual availability. Male chimpanzees, like all male animals living in fraternities, are more tolerant towards adult subordinate members of the community and juveniles. They are also more promiscuous. An ethologist observed seven male chimpanzees, one of them an adolescent, taking turns to copulate with one female without any manifestation of aggressiveness. But this item is trivial compared with what we read in our newspapers or crime records. Primate societies, like human societies, show varying degrees of permissiveness.

Sexual intercourse between mothers and sons is extremely rare. Such relations are made virtually impossible by the dominant animal's attitude to pre-adult males and by the exclusion of these from the inner circle. Heterosexual pairing is the medium through which social rank and function are transmitted. Were it to become aleatory the distinctions and divisions on which a society is based would disappear, together with its conventions and its unity. In this respect as in so many others animal societies are societies indeed.

3 *Bridging the Generation Gap*

No community can avoid inner conflict. Ethologists and biologists who ascribe such conflict to natural aggressiveness, enumerating the various situations that give rise to it in animal and by extension in human communities, ignore the dimensions of a basic social phenomenon. They project society within the individual instead of seeing it as a system with far-reaching individual and interindividual repercussions. Hierarchy spells order, but it also spells antagonism. It creates unacceptable situations and transient privileges. In primate societies statics and dynamics are provided respectively by the relation between sexual groups and the relation between age groups. There is an obvious paradox in the fact that male animals are dominant in so far as they are male and subordinate in so far as they are young. We have seen that high-ranking males enjoy social privileges which ensure their survival in both senses of the term, whereas subordinate animals, especially pre-adult males, are driven from the sheltered inner circle to the periphery where access to supplies and to females is uneasy and at best sporadic – a situation which can only increase the tensions between the ranks.

Dominant males must assert their prerogatives at all times to avoid insubordination and mutiny. While observing a population of entellus monkeys in India, scientists noted that monosexual groups were always attacking the bisexual groups. In the course of one of these forays one of the assailants abducted most of the dominant male's females. Later a gang of seven males besieged a large group for ten days, finally eliminating the dominant male and a number of youngsters. After a few days six of the gang were dispatched by the seventh, who appropriated all the females. Similar activities have been observed elsewhere. In most cases the seizure of power is accompanied by infanticide, since the privileged inner-circle juveniles tend to challenge the conqueror's rights. The disappearance of rightful heirs and the procreation of new infants establish the victor's acceptance, both sexually and socially, by the females and consequently by the rest of the community. Such modifications of the reproductive unit involve the almost total reconstruction of the basic group.

Thus the presence of reproductive and non-reproductive groups in a society is a source of unrest, for one of the many means of scaling social barriers and disrupting the *status quo* is revolt. Begging for favours is another. Subordinate animals try to obtain the dominant male's good graces in the hope of eventually acceding to power or simply mitigating the harshness of their fate. They often assume the role of 'uncle' or 'aunt' to this end. Hinde and Spencer-Booth describe the way in which mother rhesus monkeys accept the services of another female, usually one of their former playmates of inferior status, to whom they entrust their young. High-ranking mothers obtain such services by implicit threats, while those of lesser rank 'smile' or present their hindquarters to potential 'aunts' of a superior status. The advantages to a low-ranking childless female are obvious: she can partake of the high-ranking mother's priorities and enjoy her protection.

Adult male Japanese macaques make advances to very young animals, hugging and grooming, escorting and protecting them. Such behaviour is common among subordinate animals in a well-organized community, where, as a result, they will be tolerated by dominant males and their mates and so have a better chance of climbing a few rungs of the social ladder. A similar stratagem is used by hamadryas baboons. A junior male insinuates himself into a group by his submissiveness and by ostensibly avoiding any attempt to mate with the females. After a while the dominant male accepts him and gradually allows him to participate in his various activities. As the senior animal grows older and less vigorous he lets the younger take over his sexual privileges, while still retaining leadership in expeditions and in general social affairs.

Apart from such purely utilitarian behaviour there are certain ceremonial attitudes whose purpose is to mitigate antagonisms between generations. To be simply tolerated rather than attacked by high-ranking animals may lead to social promotion and permanent access to the inner circle. Effemination is typical of the ritual behaviour of aspiring adolescent or subordinate males, the object being to establish a non-aggressive relationship with the dominant male who will treat him as he would a female. To this end the lower-ranking animal adopts the female sexual stance, hindquarters offered ready for mating. This has the effect of pacifying the high-ranking animal who may even simulate copulation to show his willingness to tolerate the other's presence. The subordinate then indicates his intention of grooming the other by the conventional signal of lip-slapping (the sound which accompanies grooming, as foreign bodies found in the fur are conveyed to the groomer's mouth). The dominent male generally accepts such an offer more or less promptly, or at least refrains from chasing the subordinate away.

Such are the devices by which some animals achieve social promotion, while others succeed at least in avoiding the hardships of banishment. Mutual concessions and tolerance make for a certain amount of social fluidity, not obtrusively inconsistent with the established hierarchy and conducive to unscheduled cohabitations or successions. At times, too, a group of subordinate males may assert its rights within an enlarged social system by either splitting off from the main group, or by recruiting females, thus creating an independent basic group. Takasakiyama, whose observations have already been mentioned, reports the case of animals separating from the main community during a population increase. Those who assumed the role of dominent males were young twelve- or thirteen-year-olds originally ranking second, third and fifth in their age group. The other male members had been anchorites. The females who joined them had been living on the periphery; half of them became completely integrated, while the rest oscillated between the new and the old community. Once independent this group conformed to the pattern of the parent group, with its inner circle, periphery and so on.

Unlike such scissions, the recruitment of females is a form of abduction. Juvenile males steal young females from their mothers. The captives, who are treated with maternal solicitude, though strictly supervised to avoid escapes, soon settle down happily and groom their abductors. At this stage relations are completely asexual and are mainly directed towards consolidating affiliation. It may happen that infants of both sexes are abducted, though the juveniles tend to concentrate their attentions on their female rather than on their male captives, in order to lay the foundations for the bisexual group they will later control.

But the basic paradox of social organization can never be totally ignored, whether it is reflected in open revolt, begging for favours, scission or reconstruction. For a section of the male population must invariably – by choice or compulsion – lead a marginal existence. This section unavoidably represents a potential danger to the community, a threat to established order.

The sutdy of simian communities inevitably opens new perspectives on our own social systems and suggests stimulating parallels. Submission rituals with their homosexual implications recall the fact that sovereignty is often associated symbolically with copulation. The abduction of women and conjugal relationships with prepubescent girls and boys are common practices in some contemporary societies. And in polygamous communities a group of subordinate males is normally deprived of the right to exercise its virility. Not to mention the prevalence of hierarchy and the inequality between the sexes it involves. Yet it is misleading to stress the similarity between the customs of so-called primitive societies and our own without taking into account the notable differences between them. Primates are socially organized where relations between individuals and the reproduction and survival of the group are concerned. But otherwise their existence is entirely individual. Once an animal is weaned he has to fend for himself and can rely on no one else for the satisfaction of his needs. Feeding is an individual activity, social intervention being restricted to the enforcement of priorities at feeding grounds.

Similarly the use of anthropomorphic terms like 'family', 'leadership', or 'harem' distorts the truth. Paternity, in the proper sense of the word, does not exist in primate societies. Certain ties may exist between the nuclear couple and their progeny, but similar elements do not necessarily imply a similar structure. On the other hand in most human societies the family constitutes the basic unit.

There is a tendency either to see animal societies and our own as identical, with the former serving as model for the latter; or to consider them as two distinct variants of a biogenetic sub-structure. In my opinion they are different in that they combine individual and class relationships differently, and similar in that they are societies and as such have a number of identical requirements. Because of this latter feature they can enter into a historical series of evolutionary transformations from one into another. Thus when by force of habit I speak of a society without writing emerging from a society without speech, I do so to stress the basic unity of the progression, and not a discontinuity involved in our emergence from nature.

Georges Bataille recently observed that to accept such a discontinuity:

> is to go from one abstraction to another, and to overlook the moment when the whole of being was caught up in change. I find it hard to perceive this whole as a sequence of distinct states, and I cannot isolate the change which man's emergence provoked, from the general process of existence, from what was involved when humanity and bestiality, wrenched apart, reflected the total sundering of being. In other words existence can only be perceived in history, in mutations or the transition from one state to another, and not in a succession of isolated states.[6]

I have tried to outline the natural transition from evolution to history which primates illustrate and to describe the society of affiliation, that living example of early historical societies. I hope that this unavoidable digression will help the reader to understand the questions initially raised and enable him to assess the answers I suggest.

Part Two

The Nature of Man

[III]

A New Animal World

1 *Hominization or Cynegetization?*

The art of reinventing the past is the oldest and boldest of arts.[1] It creates a world out of next to nothing and peoples it with men and women who vanished practically without trace millions of years ago. A few hundred skull and skeleton fragments, about a thousand tons of stone and bone and roughly a hundred sites constitute more or less all the evidence we have of the emergence of humanity. On the other hand our knowledge of primate societies is based on the study of some twenty or thirty communities. We can speculate at length on something which occurred at an unspecified date in an unidentified place and was probably reenacted by various species in succession. Nonetheless, whenever and wherever it took place, it marked the traversing of that short yet immeasurable distance which divided and still divides us from beings with whom we had and still have very much in common.

The process which at a given time detached a number of anthropoids from the animal world, creating an invisible frontier, is said to have been set in motion by a sudden change of climate, flora and fauna which compelled some of our simian ancestors to abandon their rich, sheltered forest habitat for less temperate zones. As they became more and more estranged from their kin they only retained such characteristics as were still serviceable in the new dangerous and diversified circumstances. This was accomplished through natural selection, by the usual process of favourable genetic mutations and ecological adaptation. Commonplace as such a phenomenon may be, the outcome was unique, whether it was cerebral, technical or intellectual. For once this capacity was fully developed, man (or an original organic structure) emerged. Scientists are still trying to identify the decisive feature which determined the appearance of this new order of beings. Was it brain volume, bipedalism, language or the ability to construct tools? For the creature who first possessed any of these features was undoubtedly human; he continued to outdistance the rest of the animal world in great strides, adding to his physical and anatomical attributes a cultural equipment, 'a biological adaptation non-genetically transmitted and amply supplementing somatic evolution'.[2]

All these features have their supporters who are able to prove that no other species but our own possess them and that they thus represent the essential discontinuity. When it can be seen that the differences between any one trait and the corresponding trait in living or extinct primates are greater than their affinities the point is made and that trait has won the day. A pelvis revealing the requisite modifications for bipedalism, a broken stone found beside a thigh-bone, or a skull whose size might suggest that its owner could have been capable of speech are enough for scientists to declare: Here is man! The specification – biped, thinking, tool-making, talking animal – is achieved. From this point of view hominization is the emergence in the animal world of a given organ or aptitude which epitomizes a crowning (or so we believe) addition to the table of animal categories. We now know what the quality was that tipped the balance in favour of a new and unequalled anthropoid; how evolution, like a painter who adds a touch here, another there to perfect his work, modified one biological trait after another until the human race was created. The process involved a series of almost imperceptible transitions from monkey-man to man-monkey and finally to man. But at a given point in space and in time the Rubicon was crossed, with no return to the simian shore. Man was complete.

This point of view is not really satisfactory. In the first place there is always something arbitrary in the choice of one feature rather than another as the starting point for the inevitable succession of events which led up to man. Moreover, having inherited from Darwin the task of discovering how our species descended from the apes, we are none the wiser as to its ascent to man – if such terms as descent and ascent mean anything in the context. For not all the species that descended (*Australopithecus robustus,* for instance) were capable of ascending. Indeed the phenomenon known as hominization appears to have been far more complex and varied than scientists had formerly assumed.

The independent biological evolution of individual organic properties was supposed to have preceded all cultural and technical progress and to have been the necessary condition for such progress. Thus an upright position could not have been achieved nor tools constructed until the cerebral cortex exceeded that of an anthropoid. Walking had to come before running. However recent geological and palaeontological discoveries have proved that progress was not in fact achieved in the expected order. Organically speaking the size and structure of brain and limbs influenced our specific technical and cultural attainments, but historically speaking these attainments shaped brain and limbs; cause became effect and vice-versa. On the other hand the importance of social influence on biological phenomena has been seriously overlooked – or systematically ignored. The emergence of society, far from serving no other purpose than to shunt our organic development onto a different line at a moment when such a change of direction was imperative, introduced a fundamentally new element into our general development.

The unexpected discovery of technical and social evidence in the process of hominization should have been the occasion for a complete rethinking of outmoded theories and attitudes. Instead we are presented with a complex assortment of interpretations derived from the theory of natural selection, or a rehash of anthropological apologies to minimize the importance of such discoveries. But as the evidence accumulates such a revision cannot be postponed indefinitely.

That a correlation exists between an environment and the biological or social organisms within it goes without saying. But to hold ecological upheavals almost entirely responsible for the emergence of mankind is to ignore the fact that the impact of the environment varies according to the degree of evolution of a species. Even physical stature is relevant; the larger the species the greater its independence from environmental disturbances. For reasons with which we are already familiar such disturbances would not constrain the first hominids. Simians possessing identical physical and anatomical properties thrive in totally different territories, and vice-versa. Adaptation is often achieved through social reorganization without the intervention of genetic reorganization. Thus a number of scientists (including Ronald Hall) condemn the tendency to explain the behaviour of extinct human species on the basis of scanty evidence of their habitat, and to assume that such evidence can reveal the significance of a given organ or aptitude in man's radical break with the rest of creation.

The emergence of man was a long, slow process. If we still see it theoretically as a departure from non-humanity, historically we find that the state which preceded it was already human. In fact our species has a number of evolutionary derivations all distinct from those of contemporary primates. The differentiation of anthropoids occurred in the Oligocene Age, about 40 million years ago. 20 million years later, in the Miocene Age, we still shared with chimpanzee and gorilla a common ancestor: Proconsul. After that simians, such as *Dryopithecus*, adopted their present-day forest mode of existence, while hominids of the *Ramapithecus* type followed an independent course. These were succeeded by the species which 2 or 3 million years ago was represented by two types of *Australopithecus* (of which at least one was omnivorous and skilled). As for *Homo erectus*, whose remains were found in Peking and in Java, he lived 500,000 or 600,000 years before our era. Modern man is not more than 50,000 or 100,000 years old. Such a chronology can only be approximate; whether some branches overlapped and why they became extinct is uncertain. In point of fact we do not even know who was the first ancestor of the only survivor of the species *Homo,* self-styled *sapiens.* We became distinct within a process that was already specific, and hominization must have taken place in successive stages and under varying forms.

The fact that man acquired a distinct organ or anatomical feature can account neither for his scission from the animal world nor for the perdurability of the species. The acquisition itself was part of a more complex and fundamental process. Moreover the identification of such a feature has repeatedly had to be revised because its singularity proved to be questionable. Scientists then abandoned anatomical differentiation (bipedalism, brain volume, specialized forelimbs) for such aptitudes as speech and tool-making. But although the importance of language is self-evident, its significance is ambiguous. It can be defined as specifically human, or as something which includes the sign systems which primates employ for communication. On the other hand the observation of animal behaviour as well as palaeontological and ethological evidence reveal that making, or at least improvizing, tools is not an uncommon practice among both living and extinct primates. The British scientist Oakley implicitly suggests that the originality of our species should no longer be founded on such a doubtful distinction. Furthermore since the transition from animality to humanity probably occurred at various times and under various forms according to the species, there is no reason to believe that a single feature marked this transition, rather than that social organization and environmental reactions influenced the development of one feature here and of another there, of bipedalism in one place, language in another and so on. In other words there is no reason – apart from our unfounded and questionable faith in the reality of a clearly defined and unparalleled human genesis – why we should single out or exclude one characteristic rather than another.

The quest for a specific anatomical, technical or intellectual symbol of hominization reflects the tendency to project a ready-made image of man into the past and to vindicate such an image by reducing to a single solution all the possible solutions, some valid, some mere conjectures, thus obscuring a historic singularity behind organic generalizations. As if no more was required to define the essence of humanity once and for all than to win the battle of the distinctive sign. As if all that mattered was to identify the elements, not the structure of which they are part, nor the process from which they derive. This amounts to saying that if, on the basis of a single feature, it were possible to define man at a given point in space and in time then he would be defined everywhere and for all time. Such an attitude is consistent with the idea that the lesser should be judged by the greater – that human anatomy is the basis for understanding the anatomy of the ape. One would not want to contest the validity of this notion. But in the specific context of our inquiry into origins it is very easy for apparently scientific discourse to conceal a complex web of ideological values. Understanding lower forms on the basis of superior forms can too easily turn into evaluating them from such a standard. Talking, thinking man becomes implicitly thought of as the civilized white man, product of the distinction between manual and intellectual labour or between *Homo faber* and *Homo sapiens,* a distinction which, 5,000 years ago, did not exist, but which humanist and religious tradition would preserve.

This obsession with tools and technicalities, this glorification of industrialization is reminiscent of the rather limited attitude expressed by Benjamin Franklin at the beginning of the mechanical age: 'The first step was the equivalent of a first industrial revolution; for it implied not only the invention of tool-making, but that such an invention should be perpetuated as industrial tradition.' [3] This evokes an image of early man concentrating all his efforts on splitting and sharpening flint, just as the modern workman is totally absorbed and annihilated by his machine. In fact tools play a relatively minor part in the historical context.

However anthropologists are beginning to realize the incongruity of such a bias. Thus one of them writes:

> During much of this century prehistorians have confined their researches to the study of stone tools and the factual content of the Pleistocene prehistory of the 'Old World' has come to be expressed almost exclusively in techinical terms of stone-tool morphology.
>
> Considerations of activities other than tool-making tended to become a minor, semi-disrespectable adjunct to the interpretation of selected artefacts. Clearly the results of highly technical artefact studies have only a limited contribution to make to our understanding of human behaviour as a whole. [4]

A wider perspective is possible if we change the direction of our inquiries. The different characteristics or faculties relative to the process of hominization will then appear to be interdependent in their evolution and, more or less, redundant. They are links in a single chain of development. The specialization of the forelimbs was a natural consequence of bipedalism and produced the human hand, tool-making and the progressive enlargement of the cerebral cortex which made articulate speech possible; but speech was no less the result of tool-making and defensive or aggressive techniques. All these developments were simultaneous and recurrent. Quick bursts of bipedal running would accompany the grabbing of a small swift prey; they would anticipate bipedalism as such and the fabrication of weapons, traps and shelters. It is otiose to say that bipedalism or the differentiation of fore and hindlimbs were sensational events marking a point of no return, if the particular kind of bipedalism or differentiation is not specified. The simultaneous appearance and evolutionary coherence of organic and technical aptitudes reflects the system of interactions which produced, orientated and conditioned them in a given environment. In order to survive among other species the human animal tinkered with wood and stone, developed skills and tried to improve modes of communication. Above all he used his own body as material and tool, infusing it with significant gestures, coordinated rhythms and receptivity. Social cooperation assisted physical and anatomical specialization in furthering an unprecedented association between the tactile, visual and auditive faculties. Man is a maker of man. If we want a formula, there it is: he knows and understands himself as his own product and objective. During the relevant period of transition it is probable, as Marcel Mauss has said, that the essential arts were bodily arts, social and individual techniques of the body. I am convinced that a detailed study would reveal a predominance of such techniques over instrumental techniques even in contemporary non-literate societies.

But this formula, just like the others, is the product of our fascination with aphorisms claiming to have general validity. After a certain point its inadequacy soon becomes apparent, but it has some validity when considered strictly in context. Man made himself into man when he set himself up as a hunter; in other words, when he tried to acquire definite skills and means in order to relate to a given environment and was thus genetically, socially and technically transformed. He found himself in a situation where he had to cooperate with his kin *and* with the material world, if he was to perform the functions every species has to perform: reproduction, propagation and the exploitation and preservation of natural resources. Such a definition is all-encompassing. It can be historically situated; it bypasses the restrictive preoccupation with tools and sustenance; and it links up with myth, ritual and individual emotional and intellectual interactions. It also includes men – predacious or hunting – of various species which once coexisted, such as *Australopithecus robustus* and *Homo habilis;* or succeeded each other, such as *Homo erectus* and *Homo sapiens.* It distanced and distinguished them from primates, not because the latter were primates, but because they were wholly dependent on vegetation.

For millions of years man has fashioned himself a body, peopled the earth and asserted himself in his capacity as hunter. The rest necessarily followed. This view has the advantage of extending the scale and widening the grid on which our past is measured. Inquiry has been focused on too brief a period and on experiences too close to our own. Less than a tenth of our long history has been projected onto the other nine-tenths. We could do worse than to reverse the process, for it is almost inthinkable that the traces of such an experience should have left us completely unscathed.

The undomesticated animal world we now reject was, by necessity and by choice, the world of our first ancestors. They were hunters. Their lives consisted in multiplying and extending the links with this world and establishing themselves firmly within it. As today we try to penetrate the mystery of chemical reactions and nuclear fission, so these men had to uncover the secrets of bison, horse and deer. When they left the forest for the plain they were not moving from one geographical territory to another like so many anthropoids; they were submitting to the irresistible attraction of the animal world. Rather than dissociate themselves from it, they influenced it, establishing a definite relation between it and themselves. In time some of the species with whom they had coexisted in mutual indifference — as baboons coexist today with lions and antelopes — came to represent a source of supply, an indispensable element of the environment that had to be preserved and cultivated.

Their purpose, as we have seen, was achieved naturally through their own initiative. They possessed no obvious initial advantage over their potential victims, such as size, intelligence or language. The species was merely striving within a process that had already begun, deviating from the general process, while elements of history filtered through into evolution, adding a new significance to actions. We know that in such circumstances superior species are able to influence the environment thanks not only to their biogenetic aptitudes but also to their biosocial organization. The two terms of the process — organism and ecological niche — interact, responding to the impact of social organization. A group of anthropoids led the way as social behaviour became a significant part of the natural process. These bands of hominids strung together a series of activities initiated under certain circumstances, isolating them from their original context and organizing them into systematic predacity. These activities then became integrated both physically and mentally, forming, as the species perfected them, the basis of their existence. Thus man acquired the qualities that distinguish him from other species; what is more, he acquired them differently.

The full significance of the phenomenon is less in the biological division which took place within a given process than in the simultaneous reversal of this process; not so much in the specific development of organic properties as in the principle which generated it. At the very elementary level of living substance living organisms are not governed by the laws of natural selection and adaptation; and at the level with which we are concerned organisms are only marginally subjected to these laws. What occurs *in* evolution obviously depends on what happens *to* evolution. The emergence of the human species simultaneously brought into being a biological class and an original natural process.

Such a phenomenon deserves our undivided attention. We shall focus our interest on an organized activity — hunting — rather than on a specific anatomical, technical or intellectual characteristic; on a definite temporal and spatial materialization of man's being, rather than on his universalized being.[5]

We must also avoid the limitations of too great a concern with the position man occupies in the scale of creation, his uniqueness, or the size of the gap separating him from other species. Such preoccupations imply that we presume to know what is in fact unknown: the dynamics of man's genesis. This was unquestionably specific, dividing the future hominids from most other species. And this — the cynegetization and not the hominization of primates, hunters becoming men and not men hunters — is the object of my inquiry. After all, it is perhaps as important to include man in the nature he fashioned as to include him in the nature by which he was fashioned.

2 *Populations, Resources and Their Relation to the Environment*

(a) *Two kinds of equilibrium*

Such an inquiry must inevitably begin with a description of the relation between a human or prehuman population and its environment. To this end we shall posit an ideal situation (in practice rare or at best sporadic) which requires a dual state of equilibrium or harmony.

The first of these is between the number of individuals who *should* play an active part in the society and the number of those who are *able* to do so, given the amount of resources exploited and the degree of social organization achieved. A community of fifty or five hundred persons possessing a pre-established hierarchy or distribution of functions and privileges ensures its social continuity by maintaining — through breeding or recruitment — the stability of both hierarchy and population. Even in the most primitive forms of society, such as a community of hunters, the density or quantitative relation of the population reflects its demographic potential. Fluctuations are unavoidable; but a community must try to maintan a balance between demography and produce, between structure and environment, in order to survive[6]. Thus when manpower or supplies are scarce immigration is encouraged or auxiliary resources are exploited, whereas imports of one kind or another are restricted when there is superabundance.

The second state of equilibrium is between a population's various aptitudes and skills and the resources of the environment. For such an equilibrium to be achieved none of the former should be unemployed nor the latter unexploited either quantitatively or qualitatively. In this way the stability of the community's relationship to the material world is ensured; there is correspondence between activities and implements, between worker and work. Demographic stability is rightly considered in relation to the adequacy of economic supplies enabling a population to occupy a given ecological niche. But sufficiency is not the only factor, as has been confirmed by experiments on rats. A population of rodents introduced into an environment where sufficiency has been created does not increase in proportion to the supplies available. Living space and the innate aptitudes of the species appear to be indispensable factors in their rate of reproduction. There is a tendency to overlook the fact that a population, in order to thrive, must possess, besides adequacy of supplies, the aptitude to recognize, select and, in the case of human communities, produce resources as well as a capacity for social organization in order to defend and exploit a site and generally cooperate. For abundance and want largely depend on such factors. The equation organization-population equals environment-resources needs to be qualified. The relation must take into consideration a given population's potential aptitudes and the scope such aptitudes are allowed. A more inclusive and precise definition of resources is required.

They consist, on the one hand, of material elements (such as water, vegetation and chemical substances); and, on the other, of aptitudes or behaviour (such as bipedalism, systems of communication, coordination and tool-making). Further, while some resources are significant, that is to say play an important part in the collective effort or even constitute the nucleus around which the community's physical and intellectual activity is centred, others are insignificant or accessory and are only used when the need or the occasion arises. We can say that balance is achieved when a population maintains constant the ratio between its size, aptitudes and skills by focusing exclusively on significant or basic resources. For instance, if its existence depends on foraging and gathering, the only codes of behaviour, neuro-muscular relations, and experience consciously and systematically transmitted would be those concerning foraging and gathering. Territorial divisions and nocturnal or diurnal rhythms of activity are part of such a heritage. That is why a species occupying a specific niche and pursuing its hereditary activities frequently ignores a whole section of the flora or fauna which, for a different species, would constitute a basic resource. A portion of ecological or technical potential may be left fallow, since the aptitudes required to exploit it have never been developed. There is no one capable of exploiting it, for no one has been encouraged or conditioned to do so. If pre-established natural limitations are not infringed, this is not because the occasion to infringe them does not arise, but because only the organic or inorganic properties which are indispensable are transmitted and anything outside these limitations becomes unnatural and a danger to survival.

As we have said, these two states of equilibrium are rarely attained. What provokes the imbalance, and what are the consequences of trying to compensate for it?

Overpopulation is, of course, one of the causes of imbalance. In all societies or biological categories there is a discrepancy between the tendency to increase and the ability to maintain the population at a numerical optimum. The rhythm of births, recruitments or average age spans naturally adjusts to the quantity and quality of resources a society can provide at a given time. When 'productivity' increases, the procreative tendencies of the community usually follow suit. But a variety of contingencies, such as conflict with other species or geographical and geological natural boundaries, impose definite limits to expansion. In slash-and-burn agriculture a relation must be maintained between the surfaces which are cultivated at any one time and those which are cultivatable in order to get the best yield from the land. Early agricultural populations ignored this rule at their peril. The soil, starved and overrun with weeds, came to yield less and less. Similarly certain species, such as the wild horse in North America, rapidly became extinct as a result of technical advances in the art of hunting. In cases such as these a section of the community becomes redundant and is forced to find a new outlet for its activities. The propenstiy common to most reasonably prosperous societies to favour a high birth rate results in the necessity of overexploiting the environment, thus diminishing its productivity and creating an overpopulation problem. Such problems may arise from other causes, but this is the most obvious. It is also particularly enduring because changes in the rate of a population's growth are much slower than those in the rate of production, and cannot usually be speeded up without a complete restructuring of the social system. It is at such times that the supernumerary members are rejected and satellite groups are constituted; as a consequence formerly auxiliary activities and resources are exploited by these groups to compensate for the habitual activities and resources of which they are deprived. The urge to experiment, discouraged more often than not, can never be completely extirpated; when circumstances permit, it re-emerges, enabling a given group to appropriate elements that were previously shunned or ignored.

The mutations of habitat or behaviour sometimes observed in a species are generally attributed to shortage of supplies or to competition. In my opinion they are due to a store of latent riches which, in certain circumstances, a species (man for instance) is led to explore. When conditions of permanent overpopulation coincide with the discovery of such a store, unemployed activity finds on outlet and resources which were once disdained become significant. In the evolution of man predacity was the result of one of these coincidences.

(6) The supernumerary male and the threatened forest habitat
Although there may be some danger in trying to reconstruct the past by means of present events, one of the best ways of understanding how

human predacity began is to observe the habits of living primates. Among the larger apes, such as the orang-utan or chimpanzee, the males go off on scouting expeditions in groups of two to five individuals, sometimes covering great distances in search of good feeding grounds. No sooner is the site located than they proclaim their success by drumming on their chests. The females are less mobile, especially nursing mothers. But even for the males nomadism is subject to social restrictions; each animal is primarily the member of a community. When returning to the fold, even after a brief absence, a member is heartily welcomed by his kin; but should he try to enter and join up with a foreign group fighting would inevitably break out. Communal life is a necessity for these animals. It facilitates foraging, ensures regular grooming and reduces the risk of attack from beasts of prey. It is a remarkably flexible system, however. The powerful, more nomadic males who are well equipped to fend for themselves go off to the more distant feeding grounds, while the relatively more vulnerable females forage in the vicinity of the encampment; an arrangement which is to everybody's advantage. But sex distinctions have another motive besides discouraging competition for food resources and the disparity of breeding responsibilities.

In sheltered forest regions the satellite groups gravitating around affiliation societies are more or less dispersed; but in open country they congregate to form much larger bands. These associations of supernumerary, essentially non-reproductive animals have already been extensively described. But it should be noted that the division of the social body operates on two distinct levels. The sub-group of reproductive animals is naturally integrated in an established cycle of relationships and activities; but the specific roles, attitudes and privileges which define their particular rank in the hierarchy and ensure the normal development of its members, absorb their energies and restrict their horizon. The preparation of a small number of young males for the role of dominance and the servile attentions lavished upon them by 'uncles' and 'aunts', contribute to a psychological conditioning of those animals destined to remain within the permanent nucleus of the community. The females, who have every advantage in maintaining the *status quo,* exert a stabilizing influence on their adult male partners and, through these, on the whole community. Thus the dominant male – focus of general attention, acknowledged ruler and paragon, enjoying the solicitude of inferiors and the loyalty of equals – is imprisoned in the strait-jacket of tradition.[6]

The non-reproductive sub-group of supernumerary animals, on the other hand, excluded from all forms of social participation, has little chance of being integrated. Some animals may try to palliate the discomforts of their condition by resorting to various means, such as pandering for favours, submissive behaviour or, more rarely aggression; but even when their manoeuvres are crowned with success, they have great

difficulty in adapting to an integrated social existence for which they have
had no previous conditioning. The contrasting behaviour of animals living
within a community and those leading a peripheral existence has been
observed by a number of ethologists. The first tend to be assertive,
aggressive and nimble; the others, unsociable, timid and inhibited. For the
underprivileged members of these communities the answer is to explore at
large, preferably in gangs. And in such circumstances their lack of
specialization in the established activities of their community is a positive
advantage, especially as they are, for the most part, young animals whose
instinctive curiosity and inventiveness have not yet been blunted. Among
macaque monkeys, for instance, inventive behaviour has been seen, in
favourable circumstances, to produce general innovations. When these
animals were faced with the problem of conveying objects from one place
to another they would resort, briefly, to bipedal locomotion or to
swimming; at first accidental, such behaviour gradually became
customary. And we saw earlier how a group of Japanese monkeys made
the sensational discovery that sweet potatoes were more palatable when
washed. As a rule it is the young animals who inaugurate new habits. They
are apparently less wary of the unfamiliar and more prone to
experimenting with and eventually adopting new diets. The adults, on the
other hand, are too engrossed in social and environmental routine to pay
any attention to what lies beyond, so long as it does not threaten the
well-being of the community.

The diffusion of novel behaviour follows a more or less regular pattern.
It is usually initiated by a young animal as a game and promptly imitated
by his playmates. Through the channel of the mother-son relationship it
spreads to the female sub-group, whence it gradually reaches the adult
males. A change of behaviour – or of the object of a given behaviour –
only reaches the inner circle after a time-lag, to become generalized
eventually as the adolescents grow up.

There seems to be no reason why a whole mode of existence might not
conform to such a pattern, spreading from the younger members to the
whole community. Unprecedented methods of exploiting potential
resources may well have been socially organized by a peripheral sub-group
of young animals and gradually integrated by the species, quite
independent of geographical or climatic disturbances. In this respect the
rejection process of affiliation societies is at the same time a creative
process capable of radically transforming the pattern of relationships with
the material world.

On one level social division tends to induce acceptance and stability; on
another restlessness and dissatisfaction. The significance of each trend
would naturally vary with the circumstances. When supplies are adequate
or when male and female populations are suitably balanced, the
integrating, stabilizing impulse predominates and intermale aggression is

minimal. When, on the other hand, staple resources are insufficient or when mating is problematic, a section of the community becomes redundant and is rejected, with the result that it must adapt to totally different circumstances if it is to survive. The situation could be described as an endemic cleavage in the social structure which, in given circumstances, will finally result in a clear differentiation. One section of society is then compelled to emigrate and compete with different species in order to survive, while the remainder continue to reproduce the intrinsic characteristics of the original population within a relatively unchanged environment.

Primate and human adaptability is usually seen as the consequence of their peculiar physiological and intellectual capacities. I see it as the outcome of a social structure whose dynamism enables most of its members to settle within a given living space, while the others are forced to transcend it. Such dynamism is certainly active at the biological level, where a relative shortage of the essential means of perpetuating a population does not inevitably lead to extinction, and where particular associations of individuals last long enough to ensure the transmission and preservation of accumulated capacities.

Though it cannot be proved, we have every reason to believe that surplus populations, such as the groups of young single males to be found today on the fringe of primate communities, played a decisive part in the departure from the accustomed arboreal existence of the stem species from which hominids eventually emerged. Climatic disturbances certainly precipitated the transition by appreciably reducing their accustomed feeding grounds of essentially herbivorous animal populations, thus compelling them to emigrate in search of those grassy Miocene territories covered with new forms of vegetation which replaced the Eocene and Oligocene. Here mammals, including primates, from the ever-retreating forest habitat found a vast store of easy prey. In the Old World, unlike the New, there is no lack of evidence for the attempts made by primates to abandon their arboreal existence and settle on the ground. Baboon and patas monkey, vervet and macaque succeeded. So too did the ancestors of man.

First they emigrated towards the sparsely wooded marshlands dividing the thick forest from the open plain. Here, beyond the limits of their familiar habitat, the bands of supernumerary males, already accustomed to a certain amount of cooperation, were the only ones who were not too badly equipped to face the considerable risk of attack from various beasts of prey. Moreover we may assume that they were already more or less addicted to predacity and a semi-carnivorous diet. Such tendencies have occasionally been observed in contemporary primates, and would have been more pronounced millions of years ago, before man's influence on the environment had been felt. Most simians steal eggs and fledglings from nests; male baboons sometimes kill and devour new-born antelopes or other young animals; and chimpanzees do likewise with smaller species of monkey. Whereas the early primates were mainly seeking a substitute plant diet, it was the abundance of fauna, formerly consumed only accidentally, which attracted the prehumans.

Climatic upheavals created a shortage of normal supplies for which the more enterprising species were able to compensate. Ecological transformations were not causative nor did they confront the superior species with an entirely unfamiliar situation. But they aggravated anthropoid and hominid overpopulation so that neighbouring territories had to be explored to find supplementary supplies. Obviously those species, with an important reserve of more or less non-specialized individuals already accustomed to roaming abroad in well-organized bands, were alone able to undertake such expeditions. Moreover, as we have seen, such bands would be already predisposed by their age and their marginal existence to experiment and invent. Their earlier, accidental predatory experiences would, in these new circumstances, easily become habitual.

During this proto-human period of transition a source of supplies which for some time had been accidental and accessory became regular and customary. Since the reduced plant supplies were reserved for the reproductive members of the community, the non-reproductive animals severed their pre-existing links. Their carnivorous tendencies developed and they gradually acquired the skills and aggressivity consistent with such tendencies. John Crook writes: 'The change may well have corresponded to the organization of all-male bands (such as are seen among chimpanzees and geladas, for instance) into groups of hunters, and to the establishment of permanent camps, where formerly these would only have been transitory shelters abandoned at night-fall.' [7] No other group would have possessed the social and biological qualities required to confront a totally new environment and establish a different set of relationships with its inhabitants, entirely to their own advantage. But for the 'unwanted' the only hope of survival is to make accessories indispensable.

3 *Foraging for Meat*

The world of our first forefathers was a hybrid world. They stood upright but continued to swing from branches and were equally at home in marshland or forest. By day bands of young males explored the plains and scrublands at the forest edge; at night they returned to the communal arboreal sleeping sites which afforded protection from the large nocturnal beasts of prey. They were mainly herbivora, but enjoyed the occasional addition of small animals or birds, caught in play rather than in earnest.

At this stage predacity was either the stalking, capturing and killing of small animals more or less as a pastime; or it consisted in something very akin to foraging – following the trail of other meat-eaters to glean the remains of a kill. In both cases it was essential to know the habits of other animals and to be acquainted with the topography of the region. Such activities led the budding hunters further and further afield into unfamiliar territory. Moving fast and far was now a necessity. In itself this presented no serious problem; but it involved individual, organic and social mutations and amplifications when the purpose was to locate feeding grounds of one kind or another in vast, unexplored spaces. A more sustained effort was required, on the one hand because the dangers of circulating in open sparsely wooded country were greater, and on the other because foraging and hunting grounds had to be reached and abandoned between sunrise and nightfall. Moreover supplies had to be transported, and primitive tools made of sticks and stones had to be collected. Such feats could not be accomplished singly. Brute force and rudimentary weapons would afford little protection against beasts of prey. The only safety was in numbers. So long as predacity involved only attack, or the pursuit of small or very young animals, cooperation was not a necessity. It was indispensable, however, for self-defence and for exploration. Even a fierce beast of prey prefers to avoid encounters with a group of animals. The coordination of male bands acquired a technical significance.

As predacity gradually took root certain indispensable aptitudes developed. A hunter must be able to run long distances, locate prey or carrion and return punctually to the home base. He must know how to sight the prey, force it out of hiding, kill and dismember it. He must be capable of communicating the position of sites and the presence of enemies, as well as his own movements and intentions, to other members of the gang.

Higher primates are able to accomplish such tasks and to take advantage of the added benefits of meat supplies. As we shall see in the next chapter, non-human primates already used tools. Living primates are quite capable of standing upright when necessary, and of differentiating between fore and hindlimbs. Gibbons, chimpanzees and gorillas walk and run easily on their hindlegs, the body weight naturally coming to bear on a vertical axis perpendicular to the feet. Captive orang-utan sometimes stand and move clumsily on their hindlegs. Baboons, however, remain obstinately quadrupedal, though their forelimbs are already specialized and they prefer a rocky, unwooded habitat. Furthermore primates possess simple communication systems: gorillas drum on their chests; chimpanzees beat rhythmically on the ground or on tree-trunks. Diversified habitats and systematic predacity involved the intensive use of such aptitudes which consequently produced the physical and anatomical transformations which distinguish our species.

In a shared territory hominids had to distinguish between a prey, a friend and a foe. The eyes of their tree-dwelling ancestors had already undergone modifications in size and position which endowed them with stereoscopic vision and caused the nasal zone to recede. In consequence the sense of smell, by which most ground-living mammals identify their opponents or allies, grew weaker as their eyesight improved. But in some situations good eyes are not enough. In thick undergrowth, for instance, it is an advantage to be able to stand up, see over the tops of bushes and scan the surrounding country. Bipedalism, which, as we said, most anthropoids practise to a greater or lesser degree, would become a habit as a result of favourable mutations. The need to transport objects of various kinds would further develop this tendency, consolidating the relevant neuro-muscular mechanisms.

A study of half-tame macaque monkeys in Koshima, Japan, aptly confirms the above hypothesis. Here potential bipedalism developed within a behavioural system prompted by a change of diet. Between 1952 and 1962 these monkeys acquired the habit of washing sweet potatoes, an innovation which led them to venture beyond their forest habitat onto the beach. There, when some corn was provided for their consumption, a number of animals invented a method for separating the grains from the sand by washing. To wash the sweet potatoes or corn, the monkeys had to carry them to the water's edge, which they did on their hindlegs. Gradually they got into the habit of standing upright for various other purposes and for relatively long periods. By 1962 71 per cent of the community were able to walk bipedally into the sea and collect shellfish and other seafoods. Why should not proto-humans millions of years ago, in somewhat similar circumstances, have reached the same results and transmitted them from generation to generation in an environment where such modifications were required?

But there is more to hunting than seeing and carrying. A hunter must move fast: he must run. And indeed with predators, bipedilosm is associated with running rather than walking. They advance in quick dashes rather than at a slow regular pace. The remains of hominid hip-bones bear out such a theory. They are unquestionably biped hip-bones. The upper part of anthropoid hip-bones, like those of most quadrupeds, is longer and narrower than hominid or contemporary human hip-bones. The broad short human ischium makes bipedal locomotion possible by enabling the leg to stretch back to a point behind the vertical axis of the spine. Moreover the small and medium buttock muscles joined to the hip stabilize the hip-bone at each of the long strides required by such locomotion. However the early hominid ischium was longer than that of contemporary man and the buttock muscles were not sufficiently developed to serve as stabilizers and allow for a normal extension of the leg. Thus they could only advance in quick short bursts, hips and knees slightly bent, a mode of locomotion which would be too exhausting to be kept up for any length of time.

Standing upright to see further, and the bipedalism involved in pursuing game, avoiding an enemy or transporting supplies of one kind or another were not independent accomplishments. They produced secondary morphological changes and the specialization of organs, such as the human hand. Monkey prehensile forelimbs are perfectly adequate for defence or attack, for breaking off branches, carrying stones or bringing home a kill. They are differentiated in the context of predatory activities, but they are not specialized. As part of the anatomy of upright bodies they are not restricted to propulsive functions, but neither are they particularized as human limbs. Indeed the evolutionary dissymmetry of hands and feet is remarkable. Though *Australopithecus* skeleton hands definitely belong to a ground-dwelling, non-arboreal species, they are much stronger than those of modern man and the finger-joints have a pronounced dorsal curve; the feet, on the other hand, show a more pronounced resemblance to those of modern man.

Similar conclusions can be drawn from a number of clues. There is a sound basis to the belief in a connection between the evolution of the human hand and the weight of the human brain; but other considerations should not be overlooked. The structure of the skull would naturally be modified by dietary changes affecting dentition and by other facial modifications as well as by bipedalism. Thus, although the relation between body and brain weight is still approximately that of simians, the hominid's pronounced jaw, higher forehead, low inion and front-facing occipital condyles already betoken the human species. However since we will never be able to check the neuro-physiological structure of the cortex, inferences based on quantitative evidence alone – between 435 and 680 c.c. – remain largely questionable.

The brain of early hominids, skull morphology apart, does not seem to have undergone any significant modifications comparable to those affecting other parts of their anatomy. Nonetheless the human animal was induced by circumstantial changes to invent an apter mode of communication than those used by primates. A sign language of mimicry and grimaces serves no purpose in the dark or from a distance. Even acoustical signals are hard to decode against the background of continuous and variegated 'noise' predominating in the wild, especially when it is opportune to imitate the cries of certain animals in order to attract and capture them. Besides, the coordination of collective efforts requires the use of specific sounds to accompany and synchronize individual gestures. Vocal signals play a significant part in simian communities when they are on the move, or even in imposing territorial boundaries and intracommunal priorities. We are told that the cerebral cortex of the two known types of *Australopithecus* would be too small to suggest that the species was gifted with linguistic abilities. Since we know nothing of its convolutions, the number of ganglions in its nerve centres and their interconnections, or the degree of its cell specialization it is not possible to refute this. On the other hand the children of twentieth-century man are generally able to talk when they are about two years old with a 650 c.c. brain capacity. So why should not the men who lived 2 or 3 million years ago, who possessed brains of identical dimensions, have been able to do likewise? These men's mouths, formerly employed in seizing and carrying objects, were available, since the advent of bipedalism and the human hand, for specialized functions such as threatening, calling or imitating sounds. There was, here, much scope for improvement and enlargement. The evolution of the sensory muscular apparatus was undoubtedly influenced by the substitution of vocal for gestural signals. The specialization of phonatory organs and their inclusion in this physical and anatomical complex could not but affect the quality of phonic elements and their organization for the transmission and reception of orders, information or warnings.

If these men did possess the faculty of speech, it is ot the utmost significance to know what kind of speech this was. Language has two functions: a communicative, active function; and a mnemonic function whereby information derived from the material and social world is stored for later use. The communicative function makes use simultaneously and indiscriminately of verbal and non-verbal sign nuclei, and it was probably the first to emerge from the background of existing sign systems. Words embedded in vocal sequences would take shape, constitute themselves into sound groups and suggest other sounds by analogy. Their peculiarity would make them easily distinguishable from the surrounding 'noise', so that the speaker and his companions would tend to repeat them in similar circumstances and they would come to replace their non-verbal equivalents. As J. L. Austin would have put it, the language spoken by these hominids was a performative language; speaking was action – or the efficient organization of communal relations. Linguistic statement was integrated in technical and biological activity to increase man's power over nature and give a meaning to silence.

Owing to the relatively modest weight of the hominid cerebral cortex it is probable that the mnemonic function was quite independent of language, as is the case with anthropoids. Their system of communication would correspond to the requirements of a social organization similar to that of living primates. Like most other animals they were both hunters and hunted.[8]

Bipedalism, specialized forelimbs, performative speech, tool-making and an omnivorous diet are biological evidence of the human species.

Australopithecus robustus and *Australopithecus africanus* (including *Homo habilis* discovered by Leakey) correspond to the period when such organic and technical innovations occurred. These were the result of the generalization of aptitudes and behaviour patterns which existed and exist among primates and anthropoid apes. From rare they became common; from sporadic and accidental they became systematic. The human dietary system now included (besides fruit, nuts, shoots, tubers, reptiles, shellfish, insects, eggs, small animals and even baboons) carcases discarded by other beasts of prey. Antelope and giraffe remains found in prehistoric sites were probably the leftovers of lion kills, dragged home and devoured before the art of hunting made the consumption of carrion redundant. Accessory supplies and skills ceased to be accidental and were adopted by the species as regular additions to their customary diet and activities. Genetic mutations accompanied and reflected this process whereby the under-exploited and marginal technical, anatomical and intellectual potentialities of higher primates were adopted and combined to further the art of hunting. However if the terms of the natural equation organism-environment changed and evolved, the equation itself remained constant. Its sphere of action widened, its object and circumstances moved from flora to fauna and from forest to plain, but the context continued to be that of foraging and gathering.

Not only metaphorically, but even practically, predacity is a form of foraging, especially when it involves very small animals or carrion. Conversely foraging may be seen as preying on vegetation. A combination of the two ensures a greater ecological balance and a relative independence from the environment. Both animal and plant produce are less likely to become exhausted when neither is exploited exclusively, and a more stable situation prevails. On the other hand if one form of produce does become scarce there is always the other to fall back on. The human race could spread and multiply since it was able to survive in circumstances where the elements of its habitat were no longer rigidly combined. *Australopithecus* was thus able to spread rapidly into most tropical and sub-tropical regions, establishing his own peculiar mode of existence and interfering with that of other species.

Simultaneously the initial differentiation was consolidated. The first impulse was the result of overpopulation in primate communities or the fact that supernumerary individuals and groups were a consequence of the organization of such communities. A hierarchical system favouring some members and excluding others – in this case the young and the subordinate males – compelled the latter to diversify their activities and their victuals beyond the limits of their specific ecological niche. Migration without speciation, and the socialization of this migration ruled out all common animal solutions. Condemned to survive, the emigrants had to accept and adopt what they could lay hands on: subsidiary, or non-basic, resources.

As marginal groups they had little or no built-in resistance to such undertakings. For these non-reproductive males predacity was the easiest solution. It turned a biosocial differentiation into a differentiation of activities. Naturally enough they headed for the plains, where the density of edible mammals was such that experienced predacious or carrion-eating creatures could find scope for their enterprise. Like primates, proto-humans had previously coexisted with other animal species, contending for and sharing the berries and foliage of a common environment. Now these other species represented fodder for the hominids, who thus added a new dimension to this environment and appropriated it in its new form. Until then the organic differentiation of populations and their demography had been dictated by the material world's varying configurations. When the human race emerged the process was reversed and demography and social structure imposed their pattern on the material world.

[IV]

The Two Births of Man

1 From Predacity to Hunting

(a) The significance of basic resources in the evolution of man

Men became predatory when an accessory primate resource was converted into a basic resource. But the balance achieved remained precarious so long as the motives which had given rise to another major activity besides foraging persisted and this activity continued to evolve. In the normal course of events innovations very rarely replace established behaviour patterns for the simple reason that they always represent a possible threat to survival, and survival is the purpose of every species. Both tradition and heredity tend to maintain the *status quo*. A species possesses the qualities required by its mode of existence, and it cannot easily adopt a new mode requiring different qualities without the intervention of special mechanisms of readaptation.

But it was inevitable that a time would come when predacity could no longer be contained within a foraging medium. The two activities are practically incompatible, exploiting as they do conflicting attitudes and relationships to the environment and presupposing different fields of action. In the first place the attitude of foragers and gatherers is a passive one. Little more is required of them than the ability to distinguish edible plants and berries, and to pluck and consume them forthwith. All living creatures, as soon as they are biologically independent, can exercise such an activity. It depends neither on specific tools nor on cooperation. Vegetation is stationary, grows in limited areas and offers no resistance to those who would consume it. Predacity, on the other hand, involves aptitudes which range from locating the kills of other beasts of prey, to sighting, capturing and killing small game which, unlike plants, are mobile and migratory, covering sometimes great distances rapidly, and changing habitat according to the season; moreover when disturbed or attacked they are liable to defend themselves collectively. The human predator must know about such reactions and must evolve a sequence of complex manoeuvres to counteract them. His relation to other species is totally opposed to that of the forager, for he can no longer circulate peacefully in their midst, sharing their feeding grounds and watering places. A predatory population sees all other animals either as potential prey or as enemies and rivals. A lion's kill immediately attracts various types of carrion-eater who, in turn, represent for some other animal the chance of an extra meal or the compulsory sharing of the booty according to each animal's strength or skill. Whence an attitude at the same time more aggressive and defensive.

Thus the coexistence of both activities in a mixed habitat can only be a temporary, mutually restricting solution. A great deal of energy is expended in comings and goings from foraging to hunting grounds, or from the plains where game abounds to forest sleeping quarters. Such conditions inevitably limit the scope of predatory expeditions which cannot be planned simply according to the abundance of game in a given site, but must take into account the distance to be covered. Similar compulsions have been known to govern the behaviour of baboons. In Amboselli three important baboon groups went regularly by day to a particular site where water and food were plentiful but which was infested with lions. Since here the trees were few and far between, offering little or no protection from these beasts of prey, the baboons returned by night to the safety of a sleeping site one kilometre away. Hominids were probably faced with identical problems; and predacity would entail the additional complications presented by the geographical distribution of resources. Populations tend to seek a given resource in areas where it is plentiful and settle there, foregoing auxiliary resources which may be scarce or totally absent in that area. Foragers are motivated by the abundance of fodder at the expense of game, since the two rarely coincide.

Groups or individuals endeavouring to partake simultaneously of both types of resource, animal and vegetable, find that neither can satisfy their needs. On the one hand there is the basic, largely forbidden resource and on the other an accessory resource which the environment fails to provide adequately because it has been chosen for other purposes by the main body of the population. For this reason those who are compelled to adopt accessory resources and activities have no choice but to abandon their kin and constitute themselves into distinct communities. The departure from a foraging medium is a step in the direction of total integration within that of predacity; an activity which would satisfy their needs only if it could be mastered and performed more thoroughly than by their rivals in the trade. The migration of populations from the tropics towards regions where vegetation is different from that to which they have been accustomed, but where game is plentiful, furthers the transition by making it compulsory. Later, in the sub-arctic regions, meat would provide the only available winter diet, and predacity then prevails, becoming an almost exclusive activity. A dissociation which has been temporal is now spatial as well – a dissociation of material surroundings parallel to the initial dissociation of activities. The foragers continue to inhabit the temperate zones, while predatory bands penetrate further and further into the colder zones where they settle permanently.

This separation gave a specific impetus to man's evolution and marked him profoundly. It was not because they felt an urge to innovate and explore that the species dispersed, surplus members defected and organic or inorganic mutations took place. These corresponded, rather, to their need to survive and to pursue familiar activities. Proto-hominids ate meat so that they could continue to live in the world of plants, as men came to use metals to extend the range of stone. What might be called the Columbus effect – discovering America while seeking India – characterizes a number of momentous historical ventures.

(b) A major division

The urge to improve predatory methods and skills and overcome the obstacles of a material and psychological foraging background severs the last links. The new subsidiary activity which circumstances had created has to be turned into a full-time activity. For centuries men had tried to surpass the other beasts of prey with whom they had to contend. Finally they surpassed themselves to become a different kind of predatory animal – a hunter.

The major discovery in this process was that a carcase could be produced at will. Men already knew how to kill small animals and were accustomed to eating the remains of large ones killed by beasts of prey. The two activities merge when the methods employed for the first are transferred to the second. Now everything has to be on a much larger scale. Men pursue and attack herds of huge and often extremely agile animals who travel through diversified regions and are dispersed over vast areas. These kills cannot be consumed on the spot but have to be dismembered and transported. New methods and implements are invented to dissect and preserve the carcases and to make separate use of skins and bones that now litter the dwelling site. Social cooperation develops in two directions. As long as men were predatory they cooperated to defend themselves against the beasts whose kills had to be consumed where they lay. For this the systems of communication employed by foragers were still adequate. As hunters – though individuals may occasionally have operated singly – they usually work in bands which have to be carefully organized, each member's activity having to be related to that of the other members who assist and protect each other. Here a new kind of cooperation is required. Success and survival in hunting expeditions depend on the preliminary evaluation and standardization of the physical and intellectual ability of those taking part. It is an enterprise involving concerted action. And man now starts out on his man-making career. His arts and implements enable him to make substantial use of animal supplies, besides eating the flesh, and these prove to be more than a substitute for plants. Henceforth human communities can migrate to regions where vegetation is scarce and settle in a diverse but no less viable habitat.

Hunting populations – one might even say species – diverge from the predatory groups. Their art is more specialized and their activities are socialized rather than individual. Hunting becomes a distinct, basic occupation. As predacity emerges from its foraging background to evolve into hunting, the discrepancy between male and female activities increases; indeed the discrepancy was an inevitable condition of this emergence. One person could not combine satisfactorily two activities requiring such different aptitudes as foraging and hunting. The art of hunting could only achieve the level of perfection on which its success depended if it was pursued exclusively. A parallel can be drawn here with the potter's art, practised at first as a sideline by cultivators, which had to become the exclusive activity of a section of the population before it could reach a degree of perfection. Hunting was an eminently male activity; not so much because it made demands on physical strength and endurance as because its pioneers happened to be the all-male sub-groups of socially rejected individuals. The women, on the other hand, had continued to maintain the traditions of the species. While hunting evolved they pursued foraging activities, which did not necessarily exclude 'gathering' small prey or devouring the remains of a kill. What takes place is not, as is usually believed, a simple division of labour where the sexes specialize in two different activities while exploiting a single produce. Here the two developments in a single cycle diverge, much as in the case of two related species where one lives under water and the other, having acquired the necessary respiratory organs, on land.

Gathering is a meticulous, individual, relatively primitive activity. Hunting, as we have seen, involves a complex sequence of premeditated, organized, collective actions requiring a certain degree of evolution. Alex Comfort observes that: 'Over a period that began 350,000, and ended 11,000 years ago, man had two main occupations, gathering food *like the great anthropoid monkeys* [my italics], and hunting like the Pygmies and Eskimo.'[9] The hunter is in certain respects as distinct from his foraging, gathering mate, as a human being from a non-human. The segregation of the sexes in their respective resources and skills might be compared to the distinction between two systems of behaviour, or two languages such as French and German, rather than to the differences of accent and idiom found in different social strata, reflecting class distinctions and by extension division of labour. It created a permanent non-communication, more than a simple lack of communication. It enabled a type of behaviour and activity which had no precedent in the animal world to take root, to resist the passage of time and to reflect man's peculiar image.

(c) The art of catching and the art of killing

The first humans begin to eat meat (mainly carrion left over from another animal's kill as a simple extension of their foraging habits. They are no more selective than they had been in their plant diet. Baboons, for instance, live on at least fifty different kinds of plant, eating the fruit, the buds and the shoots. Hominids appear to have been equally eclectic. The spoils from two African sites dating back 500,000 years — a period of transition in most respects — include three varieties of monkey, two of carnivora, three of sheep, three of giraffe, some buffalo and a lot of antelope remains as well as those of rodents, birds and tortoises. The transition from foraging and predacity to hunting is marked by a greater selectivity.[10] Hunting populations tend to concentrate on a limited number of species whose habits they observe, while perfecting the methods that will give the best results in each particular case. At the famous Chou Kou Tien site near Peking only the remains of carnivorous and ungulate mammals were found, of which about two-thirds were deer of two kinds. Near Torralba in Spain elephants, wild bulls and horses were the only animals hunted. In a cave dwelling in Croatia dating from the Aurignacian period 90 per cent of the bones belonged to bears. Mammoth accounted for most of the game hunted in southern Russia and central Europe. At Solutré in the Dordogne the remains of 100,000 horses have been discovered, while it seems that at a later date reindeer was a more popular prey in the same locality. Though such evidence is not conclusive hunting does appear to become more selective, and by the time *Homo sapiens* appears a single type of game satisfies all the population's needs. Even the animal kingdom is split up, divided and differentiated.

Specialized skill is the result of the specialization of resources. The operations involved are perfected and organized when they become established. The hunters develop their art methodically and evolve a coherent complex of knowledge and behaviour. It is quite true that: 'Human hunting is made possible by tools, but it is far more than a techinique, or even a variety of techniques.'[11] Snaring, for example, opens a wide ranged of possibilities. Since it is purposefully directed against a restricted variety of animal species it has a significant impact on these as well as on the men who invented it. Its purpose is capture, which is more effective than attack and requires more refined methods to overcome the victims' agility and awareness. Nets, pits, traps and pegs must be first invented and then operated to immobilize or restrict the prey. The kill must be carefully timed to avoid unnecessary risk. Not so long ago Eskimo were still hunting the brown bear on the island of Kodiak by planting a javelin in the ground and holding down the tip with one foot so that the onrushing animal was impaled on it; sometimes they fixed a guard on the javelin to keep their victim at a safe distance. The brown bear is the largest living carnivore, weighing sometimes up to 800 kilos against the

Eskimo's 65. The obvious advantage of such a method, apart from its efficiency, is its relative safety. Trapping and snaring include attack and defence in a single operation. They require a knowledge of animal habits: the paths they usually follow, how to attract or disperse them, the density of herds and bands as well as their organization and composition. Such a store of knowledge can only be acquired over a number of generations and transmitted through language, myths and rituals that constantly evoke and enrich it. Snaring involves a technical and intellectual ability which shows that hunting is more than self-control and endurance; it is predominantly a question of cunning which enables the weak to dominate the strong and adds to reality the new dimension of feint and fiction.

Direct attack is a matter of dexterity and precision. It can be more exerting than rewarding to throw stones, shoot arrows or thrust a spear; missles are liable to miscarry and the wounded prey to escape. Moving or stationary targets have to be carefully sighted; familiarity with the victim's anatomy and reactions is essential in order to locate the most vulnerable spot and avoid excessive risk; the speed and trajectory of weapons has to be calculated precisely. Besides training for fitness and precision, contemporary hunting populations spend a great deal of their time observing and dissecting the animals they hunt. In the Aleutian Islands the practice target is divided into sections named after parts of animal anatomy, and painted red and black to represent the fur and the blood.

If animals are indiscriminately trapped, poisoned and slaughtered, whole species would be threatened with extinction. In order to avoid such an eventuality hunting populations 'cultivate' game by allowing it to breed. Such an attitude is totally foreign to predacity. It reflects a high measure of foresight and self-control as well as a conscious, premeditated relation to the environment which is still current today and probably emerged at a very early date. Taboos have often fulfilled the function of preserving a population's livestock by forbidding the slaughter of animals under a certain age or of females with young, and by enforcing seasonal restrictions.

There is evidence that in the last Ice Age hunters had devised a method for capturing whole herds of animals by driving them over cliff tops. Tasmanian tribes operated in a somewhat similar fashion when they encircled herds in a given area and then closed in and mass-slaughtered them; here they soon realized that in the long run the result would be fatal and the practice was restricted by taboos. An irreplaceable source of supply was thus preserved from total destruction. We will probably never know whether similar taboos controlled the populations of the last Ice Age, but it is not unreasonable to suppose that they did. For hunters tend, as a rule, to respect the habits of different species and to preserve them from extinction. Tongouse and Aleutian populations, among others, will not cross the frontiers of what they consider to be a certain animal's rightful territory without trying to appease it by uttering words in a special language which they believe the animal can understand; or they make use of frightening devices to subdue it. The systematic observation of animal behaviour which such attitudes reflect is far from exceptional. A band of Tongouse hunters, seeing a water-fowl disappear into a hole in the ice and then re-emerge from another hole, captured the fowl and attached it to a long thread in order to check if what they had observed was correct; after which they killed it and submitted the carcase to a series of tests to see what kinds of parasites it might have collected in its underwater trip. They are also in the habit of keeping young animals, ostensibly as pets for their children; but it is obvious from the attention with which adults observe these animals that the main purpose is the acquisition of a better understanding of their habits.

Furthermore it was through hunting that social cooperation was initiated. Between hunters information has to be clearly expressed and promptly understood; communication must be realized by means of a standardized code. Postures and gestures acquire a collective significance and the human body is considered in the light of the common purpose. Physical and intellectual indoctrination start as soon as a boy can walk, and continue until he has become a fully integrated member of the community. The hunter's art is one with which he identifies and that sets him apart. He is no longer a specialized predatory animal, a being gifted with hereditary aptitudes peculiar to his kind. He is a man in his own right, conscious of the fact and of the distance that separates him from other men — and from women.

2 Denatured Man

(a) Learning from anthropoid tool-makers

As yet I have intentionally refrained from discussing the tools which accompany and reflect man's evolution, symbolizing, for those who made them as well as for those who now contemplate them, his new relationship with the environment. I thought it would be more helpful first to set the scene in which they appeared.

Though hunting and tools fit perfectly into the general evolutionary cycle, they are represented as having severed our links with the common, natural cause to set us up in the distinctive solitude of which we are so proud and so afraid. 'Employment of tools appears to be (man's) chief biological characteristic, for considered functionally they are detachable extensions of the forelimbs' [12] writes K. P. Oakley. But this definition refers only to a certain kind of tool and omits all the other contrivances such as snares, nets, traps, poison and fire which can hardly be said to extend any part of the human anatomy. This exclusive connection between tool and hand (the latter being in fact, from an evolutionary point of view, an extension of the former) is the projection of a simplified form of more recent craftsmanship into the past. Moreover the deliberate refusal to consider implements made of any material other than stone – whence the various Stone Ages – results in scientific attention being focused on certain objects because they were fashioned from a substance capable of resisting the effects of time and not because of their intrinsic significance.[13] The term 'Stone Age' is no more comprehensive a definition of man's achievements at a given time than would be terms such as 'Atomic' or 'Plastic Age' of the present. Such an attitude restricts our outlook to a single facet of human activity considered from a technological point of view, without any reference to the amount of experience and cooperation it required or to the needs it satisfied. It is surely more apposite to try to see these tools as part of a complex system of behaviours and skills, rather than to compare them to the contemporary mechanical devices of which they are supposed to be rudimentary examples; for a tool ceases to be a tool when removed from its context. The next step, then, is to find out what this context was.

Predacity estranged hominids from their foraging kin and encouraged an attitude of creativity and experimentation. Pre-existing subsidiary resources and activities were exploited and adopted; among these were improvised tools. For tools were not invented by man. They can be found among the so-called inferior species. Young baboons carry sticks and branches; they are quite capable of breaking off a twig to extract larvae from a hole. They handle and examine unfamiliar objects or displace a slab of rock in their search for edible insects. Orang-outans use sticks to dig insects out of their nests and eat them. Chimpanzees do likewise, breaking branches to the required length. Sometimes they introduce a long blade of grass into a bee-hive and then suck off the honey on it. Their young learn these tricks by observing and imitating them.

At Libera Creek chimpanzees have been known to crack open coconuts by hammering them with stones. Others use leaves as cups or squeeze them out after soaking them as sponges when they want to drink. A group of ethologists were able to film a band of chimpanzees confronted with a stuffed leopard. Once they had overcome their initial fear the animals greeted the intruder with an outburst of highpitched or raucous cries. The main body then rushed forward, and were soon joined by the more timid members who had first taken to flight. They pelted the leopard with improvised missiles while stamping and drumming on the ground. Some used standing saplings to flagellate their enemy; most of them stood on their hindlegs using their forelimbs to wield or throw weapons. Whereas in normal circumstances violence is restricted to threatening jestures, here they were openly aggressive, aiming accurately at the leopard's head round which they had grouped themselves in a rough semicircle. Chimpanzees living in marshland territories are generally more skilful than their forest-dwelling brothers. They take greater pains when preparing weapons, stripping the leaves off branches two or three metres long. All meat-eating primates and anthropoids improvise and make use of some kind of tool, even if their ability to do so is unsophisticated. Tools are definitely not the prerogative of man.

To obviate the distressing effects of this revelation a nice if questionable distinction has been imagined: the prerogative is in fact at one remove from *using* tools; it consists in *making* them. Moreover 'Tool-making requires a higher order of intelligence than their use,' K. P. Oakley reassures us.[14] But this projects the functional sub-divisions of an industrial age onto a background where they are meaningless. Of course there is a difference between picking up a stone or breaking off a branch in self-defence, and handling a tool as a carpenter handles a hammer or a pair of pliers. The stone or the branch is not a tool until it is used as such. The gesture that singles it out from all other stones or branches, that hurls or wields it, is what endows it with a purpose and simultaneously includes it in the category of tools. It turns the branch into an extension of the body not the tree and invests the inert stone with movement. Instead of being part of the landscape these objects are now resistant, heavy, flexible or sharp objects. Tools, however rudimentary, are always made in that they are the result of an effort and the transformation of raw material. What is an untooled stone used to sharpen a stick? And the being who uses the stone? Is he using a tool when he handles the stone? Is he making a tool when he sharpens the stick?

Such questions are pertinent. Prehistoric stone implements are not easy to identify. The bits of broken flint examined by the archaeologist could be man-made or the result of some entirely independent accident. The only reason for supposing that they are the product of deliberate action is their presence in large quantities near human remains. They are remarkable not so much for their individual shapes as for their accumulation in a given spot. For instance at the Sterkfontein site in South Africa some of the implements are merely untooled river pebbles. Yet they must have answered some purpose since they were transported all the way from the river bed which is several miles distant. The simple fact of piling them up may have had some now inexplicable instrumental significance. We cannot assume that beings capable of carrying out such an exacting task were only able to use improvised tools. They must surely have fashioned simple implements from bone or wood. A branch or twig is rarely of the exact shape or size required for a given purpose, or it may be partly rotten. Some adjustment is always necessary before it can be put to adequate use. Is it legitimate to doubt prehistoric man's ability to make such an adjustment? There is no lack of evidence to dispel this doubt in more recent European sites. Moreover Australian tribes currently combine the use of wood and stone, felling trees or making wooden tools with the help of sharp stones. In a number of sites implements made by splitting or breaking bones have been found, and surely it is as much a technical feat to cut wood or bone as to cut stone. If evidence of the former activity is less common this is owing to the material's greater fragility rather than to its insignificance to men who could hardly have done without it. We must discard the notion of man the tool-maker as the product of a sudden flash of inspiration which, from one moment to the next, turned a sub-human being into a fully-fledged human. The distinction between fabricated and improvised tools is not an easy one to make, especially when the archaeological data are inconclusive.

Man's instrumental ability is simply the development of a feature which anthropoids and primates failed to develop for want of a purpose. In this respect the chimpanzee is closer to man than the macaque monkey, for instance, though the latter has achieved a higher stage of social and physical evolution. Tools, as such, do not necessarily reflect the evolutionary progress of a species; the activities and resources which made them indispensable should always be taken into account. They are not extensions of the human body. When hunting evolved from predacity they acquired a general function, a permanent value and a necessary structure consistent with the anatomy of man. An American anthropologist writes: 'Humans did not become human and then learn how to hunt other animals but already were hunters and simply altered their methods of hunting in conjunction with the acquisition of ideas that permitted the use of tools and, later, their manufacture.' [15]

The invention and the use of tools – including sticks and stones – is part of a process of adaptation to a complex of organized activities and knowledge. Within this complex tools play a relatively minor part; improvised weapons and implements satisfy most current needs. However the consequences are boundless. For once tools have been integrated into the complex, they influence the development of the body which manipulates them. To survive in its social and material habitat it is no longer enough for this body to be fed and tended and for its various needs to be satisfied. Its agility and power must be exploited as a deliberately cultivated resource now that it has to contend with other species. The individual and collective force opposing forces of nature depends entirely on physical power and agility, carefully achieved and maintained. The human body emerges from an undifferentiated background as a term of reference, or as one of the terms in an equation in which the environment provides the other. This is where man outstripped his anthropoid kin from whom he had never ceased to learn and borrow.

(b) From contrivance to nature
Tools probably evolved in two stages; first they were popularized, then diversified. Ronald Hall, listing the various tools employed by animals,

classifies them as domestic tools used as gestural extensions in order to reach awkwardly situated objects, and aggressive tools for attack and defence. The former are more or less common to most species; the latter are exclusive to primates and anthropoids. It is not surprising that hominids, living in the circumstances we have outlined, should adopt and perfect such tools. Here bipedalism was a considerable asset. A quadruped can handle a domestic tool to cut meat, break bones or even dislodge a small prey when he is squatting down. But it requires not only bipedalism but a quick, easy gait and a sure aim to make efficient use of aggressive weapons. These qualities are the result of specialized forelimbs.

The oldest excavated sites reveal that tools were popularized in the form of sharp, naturally splintered flints, rough axes made out of large, barely modified bones, pebbles and small sharp-edged slabs of rock. The stone piles found near living quarters or temporary camping sites were probably missiles kept in store against a possible intruder in sparsely wooded regions where the more usual impromptu defensive weapon, a branch ripped off a tree, would not be available; these communities may well have provided themselves with clubs into the bargain. But aggressive and defensive skills were still restricted to such practically untooled objects.

The earliest evidence of man's emergence is the existence of rudimentary tools generically known as Stone Age implements. These were conceived and fabricated for a given purpose. Bits of quartzite found in the High Kalifa basin eighty kilometres north of Elizabethville show traces of hammering along one edge and in some cases over the whole of one face. According to the Abbé Breuil these sharpened stones were used for cutting wood. Their uniformity and functionality are remarkable; stone has evidently become a well-tried raw material.

But as hunting evolves into a full-time occupation, tools tend to be more diversified. It is their diversification rather than their fabrication which is peculiar to man – the term here standing for human *and* for male, since these tools were the work of all-male cynegenetic bands. Their range continues to increase as occupations grow more varied and animal by-products are systematically exploited. Stones are no longer merely heavy objects to be used in defence and attack. A splinter of flint cuts through flesh and bone, or it can serve for chopping, grating and scooping. With such a tool kills are skinned and quartered, and the parts that cannot be consumed on the spot are carried off for later use instead of being wasted. Bradawls, scrapers, cutters and polishers are invented and put to specific uses. With the help of burins, soft stone, bone, horn and wood can be fashioned into implements. Axes, javelins and choppers in Asia, complete this list. Some of the earliest examples of such artefacts were found near the remains of Peking Man. Henceforth evidence of a whole range of skills can be found wherever man has left traces of his presence on earth. Methods and styles vary according to the population, the region and the animal most usually hunted. Hunters specialize and perfect formerly accessory aids till they become indispensable instruments which add an unsuspected dimension to their actions and to their world. More than a simple organic extension or an isolated technique, tools constitute one of the links in a chain of social and intellectual developments.

The modified anthropoid anatomy is eminently suited to its new cycle of activities and to the changing environment. But the intellectual, perceptive and technical qualities required by the hunter's art make a further series of modifications necessary. We tend to think of the process as having occurred in reverse order, because it was so totally successful; that is we think that the hunter's art was the result of man's modified faculties. But palaeontology is there to correct us. Bipedalism, the specialization of the human hand and the increased volume of the brain develop non-biological faculties by affecting the nervous and muscular systems. These faculties which are natural to human beings today were not natural to the men who lived millions of years ago. In fact these men created them: what one man contrives becomes another man's nature.

All anthropoid primates have prehensile forelimbs, but only in man are they not propulsive as well. Prehension operates by means of the respective position of the fingers, the palm and the foream when holding an object or stretching out to seize it. The hand has to grasp an object firmly and keep it steady. For manual activity firmness and precision of grip are combined. The firm grip steadies the object by clamping it between the partially flexed fingers and the thumb; precision is achieved by gripping the object between thumb and finger-tips. The muscles which control firmness and precision are distinct and more or less coordinated according to the species. Baboons and chimpanzees use the thumb and forefinger with more dexterity than most men when extracting a scorpion's sting or a thorn from their flesh, but their thumbs are relatively weak and too short to enable them to grasp an object firmly.

The diversity and intricacy of man's manual activities gradually modified the bone structure of his hands and the nerves and muscles exercised when seizing prey, a tool or a piece of food. The human thumb in particular, which is completely opposed to the flexed fingers, allows for the meticulous operations required by a hunter, such as setting a trap, fashioning weapons or dismembering a carcase. The hand is now under complete control and the range of its achievements is extensive. The development of the human pelvis which enables man to stride along on his two hindlegs and cover great distances is, in comparison, a minor evolutionary event.

The human brain was begotten by the human hand – or, more precisely, by hunting.[16] Hunting created an interruption in the evolutionary cycle where, even after the advent of predacity, the brain had remained akin to that of primates and anthropoids. The capacity of modern man's skull is 1200 to 1500 c.c.; that of the skull of *Homo erectus,* who lived about 500,000 years ago, was between 710 and 1100 c.c. Admittedly the shape of this skull was different. The brain pan was long and flat and the frontal bone formed an uninterrupted ridge over the eyes, as with gibbons and chimpanzees. Notwithstanding this morphological parallel, the brain it contained was the size of a highly intelligent modern man's. In this respect at least Java and Peking Man were our contemporaries.

The development of the cerebral cortex is hard to explain. It is due in part to the greater height of the body. On the other hand the stricter control of body reactions, of aggressive and expressive gestures, has a definite impact on the development of the tonsils and also on the 'domestic' sections of the cortex to which these are connected. But the human brain is not remarkable so much for its size as for its distinctness. Since *Australopithecus* the number of brain cells has considerably increased, but this increase was not accidental. In monkeys the areas of the cortex that correspond respectively to the fore and hindlimbs are approximately the same size. With *Homo erectus* the areas governing the fingers and thumb already show a marked predominance. The neuro-muscular areas receiving tactile information from the fingers and controlling their flexion and extension are now distinct and coordinated. Developments and mutations in one area of the brain extend to neighbouring areas so that new neuro-physiological regions can be exploited. Most of the available surfaces of a monkey's brain correspond to its neuro-muscular functions. The evolution of these functions in man led to the subsequent development of adjacent areas of the cortex, facilitating their association with skill, memory and speech.

The division of the brain into two hemispheres, the dissymmetry of the left and the right, and the coordination of peripheral neuro-muscular transmissions make possible a system of mental operations of baffling complexity. Its development was simultaneous with that of cynegenetic arts and weapons, which undoubtedly stimulated it more than we generally believe. The split which was concurrent with these activities, when the species set out on its quest for an independent means of survival, has left its mark on the human intellect. The persistence of logical dualism, our systems of communication and our subdivisions of space and of time are some of its manifestations. Though it is not a genetic datum, in that it is not a spontaneous property of living matter, it is difficult to see what else it is, since the human brain, the whole human organism, the differentiation of human fore and hindlimbs and of the right and left hand establish and summarize it. Significant sequences are abstracted from the perpetual flow of information and from the unbroken thread linking one generation to another; they create not discontinuity but close-ups which enable man to learn, understand and survive in a world he fashions in the process of fashioning himself. The linguistic area autonomously projected on the cortex increases as man evolves. Hunting populations must know how to describe and connect events and how to name the different animals, tools and materials they deal with. Performative speech evolves and develops to include the cognitive speech required by more complex relationships. Accumulated experiences merge, technical and social activities are coordinated and man discovers his own identity as he discovers speech. Through speech, or the link between will and deed, time appears on the scene as communal history, lending voice to the absent, uniting past and present and setting the present in the context of the past. This is indeed a major turning-point, a departure from the discontinuity that governs the animal world where generations disintegrate and populations disperse when their ecological basis is removed. Conceptual thought is a flimsy acquistion in comparison. But two speciations were necessary — *Homo erectus* and *Homo sapiens* — before language could take permanent root.

3 *The Human as Element and the Human as Structure*

These facts are common knowledge and generally serve to prove how eventful man's emergence was. Yet the precise frontier between primate and man remains as elusive as ever. There is and there will always be a missing link in the chain connecting ape-men to modern man via men-apes. When the biological, intellectual and technical aspects of the process are abstracted, the sequence appears uninterrupted and the breaks in continuity caused by the activities responsible for such aspects become no more than notches on a gauging-rod. Nonetheless the impression persists — providing fuel for scientific dissension — that the transition from hominids, who are not entirely human, to human beings, who notwithstanding their many anthropoid characteristics are definitely not anthropoid, has not been satisfactorirly clarified. Of course there are ways and means of dispelling this impression by stressing, for instance, the significance of tools, intellectual aptitudes or organic mutations; or by attempting to gauge the precise distance between men and apes through (usually unsuccessful) experiments with chimpanzees, such as teaching them to talk and to solve mathematical problems. But in fact this impression is justified. In a generally anthropoid world the humanity of hominids is unquestionable, whereas men preserve anthropoid characteristics within an ensemble of characteristics which is not anthropoid at all. Such reversals are not unusual. Significants events — the Renaissance, the Reformation, the French or the Russian Revolutions — had a variety of beginnings, but this does not prevent us from dating them precisely for the sake of records and anniversary celebrations. Likewise the genesis of man was twofold.

Neuro-physiologically, for instance, first the localized neuro-muscular systems were differentiated, then the cerebral cortex and specific modes of coordination. In the sphere of linguistic communication the phonetic units of performative speech were integrated by a system of non-verbal signals, before cognitive speech could associate the non-lexical elements within a specific system of rules and codes. Finally, where tools are concerned, they were generally used and improvised long before they were deliberately fashioned and then differentiated.

The first birth in hominid development is that of the specific animal which tried to make common what had previously been exceptional and to concentrate that which had been diffuse. Occasional anthropoid activities and achievements such as pursuing game, improvising tools, bipedalism, exploration and invention, or emitting and receiving signals, are adopted on a regular basis by a group of individuals and converge into a powerful cooperative system which dominates the elements which had previously defined their world. Predacity is the background against which attitudes and relations merge, reinforce each other, become more frequent and extend the range of genetic mutations that would otherwise have failed to develop. On the surface nothing or next to nothing is changed, but in fact everything is different. The organic structure and new dietary habits of *Australiopithecus* reflect this transformation and the specific process from which it arose. Humanity, entirely dominated by problems population expansion has created, is still part of the animal world. The process set in motion is not yet irreversible; the way back into the primate world is not cut off.

At his second birth man perfects the aptitudes, methods and organs he has inherited from other species, coordinates them and turns them into specifically human aptitudes, methods and organs. With *Homo erectus* and *Homo sapiens* specialization begins. Men are no longer both prey and predator, forest and marshland dwellers, plant- and meat-eaters. Animals have become a valued source of natural supplies instead of being equals and rivals. Moreover now that male energy is entirely concentrated on the art of hunting, existence depends almost exclusively on the animal world. Animals provide food, clothing, artists' material, calendars, topics of conversation; timetables and seasonal migrations are planned according to their habits. The whole rhythm of everyday life is made to coincide with this vital preoccupation.

Since it was biologically possible to eat meat, to capture and devour animals, men were led to capture and eat each other.[17] Anthropoids are not aggressive or fierce by nature, but such features are highly developed in the hunter. Evidence of cannibalism is quite extensive in prehistoric sites; it was a natural development of hunting. The extinction of all but two hominid species is usually attributed to the impact of climatic alterations on flora and fauna. Yet it is more probably the result of a dynamic coexistence. The more evolved species were well equipped to hunt those who were still at the stage of unskilled predacity and had relatively primitive technical and social means. Or perhaps the less adventurous communities were simply starved to death as a consequence of their neighbours' superior ability to capture and kill a common prey. The after-effects of glaciation and the ebb and flow of populations merely concluded a lengthy process. Be that as it may, the physical and anatomical, technical and social non-primate human constitution which hominids had retained dissolved, to re-emerge transformed within the physical and anatomical, technical and social non-primate human constitution. Henceforth the consequences are irreversible.

We have been following step by step a process of division that took millions of years and is of incomparably greater significance than accumulation or selection. This process initiated a sequence of incompatibilities, but it was at the same time a consequence of their solution. Innovations were cancelled by interruptions and divisions which created other innovations enacted by beings who concentrated all their energy and intelligence on making accessories into necessities and on preserving or transforming that which was condemned to disappear. Collecting and storing animate and inanimate objects, standardizing and generalizing arts and artefacts discovered by accident, integrating them into everyday life is often a desperate undertaking, but it is always creative. The qualities we now possess and the medium in which we live are what our hominid ancestors were strenuously pursuing – they literally created them. It is misleading to maintain that these things were revealed to them, or that they were dislodged from their forest habitat by geophysical upheavals alone. We tend to believe that it is our fate to fight against nature, dominate the elements, flora and fauna. In fact the conflict is man-made. The hunters contrived to dominate their prey, but this prey had a vital or rather a human significance for them; their entire biological, psychological and social constitution depended on it. The opponents may have varied but such conflicts have always existed. They occur wherever a portion of humanity is forced to construct its own reality, outstrip existing conditions, escape the past and assert itself by opting for the future. Such is the price of survival.

[v]

From Natural Selection to Natural Division

1 *Inversion of the Environment-Population Relation*

Divisions like the division between hunters and gatherers are recurring phenomena which we shall now try to define. The evolution of a species depends on the combined action of mutations and the laws of heredity; in other words, on the integration of accumulated random physical and chemical processes by regular organic processes. A given species is always liable to revert so long as it has not fully emerged. After that it is irreversible: the blueprint of its past biological developments will be faithfully reproduced in the future. Its constitution is the result of accidental mutations adopted and standardized; its evolution corresponds to reversals of values within a generally unvarying structure. Genetic reproduction ensures its permanent constitution, while selection influences the course of evolution by adapting this structure to environmental conditions. The diffusion and natural evolution of organic matter which we call survival is in fact the uninterrupted production of life. The sub-divisions of the animal world correspond to migrations in space and in time reflecting the tendency, natural to all species, to explore and inhabit a different ecological niche. The survival and productivity of specific individuals is determined by the differential reproduction of favoured qualities enabling them to adapt to a new environment by appropriating unusual aptitudes: the ability, for instance, to live under water rather than on land, to be active by night instead of by day or to eat meat instead of plants. At the same time socially determined reproductive differences exert an equally powerful influence and reflect the behaviour of socially organized beings rather than their genetic structure.

For although intra-social mechanisms naturally involve genetically similar individuals, they introduce an additional factor to their relative chances of survival and procreation. Hierarchy, for instance, which creates within a population differentiations that are indistinguishable as regards their genetic properties, adds a significance to objects, physical or sexual stimuli and to living space which varies with each sub-group, so that something which may be normal and pleasing to one is unnatural and repulsive to another. Individuals are permanently marked by such compulsions which effectively divide the population into categories, each with its ingrained reactions. These categories may well be the result of concerted allocations of tasks and activities, since in many species, particularly mammals, neither sex nor age are the common factor distinguishing such groups.

By creating both a social heterogeneity in the relatively undiversified genetic structure of a species, and an intra-specific homogeneous distribution of individual functions, despite genetic diversities (e.g. sex differences), these social forms enhance organic potentials in general while furthering specialization. Thus in the course of evolution they have had a stabilizing effect, notably on population growth. Their influence on primate, anthropoid and hominid populations has been greater than that of differential sexual reproduction. It enables a single species to adopt and transmit the different social structures of various species. It facilitates the simultaneous exploitation of a series of successive social factors or combinations of factors, rather as though established customs could acquire experience through the conflation of different customs conceived in different places and at different times by biologically distinct beings. Jacques Monod asserts that the role of telenomic action in determining the course of natural selection becomes increasingly significant as organization improves and makes organisms less dependent on the environment. So much so that this role could be seen as conclusive for superior organisms whose survival and reproduction depend primarily on behaviour.'[18] He also claims that in such societies selection no longer operates, or at least that it is no longer 'natural' in the Darwinian sense.[19]

But although we have broken away from a section of the biosphere which is common to most animal species, we have come to depend on less obvious sections in the very act of recreating our direct material surroundings. To see this change as a sign of independence is to consider it only from a negative point of view as a departure from a former state. Seen from another, more significant angle it is the culmination of an evolutionary process where behaviour now mediates between organism and environment. The factors responsible for such a process are well known. First, an average life-span extending beyond the age of sexual fecundity. This widens the gap between one generation and the next, reducing the rhythm of population growth and genetic mutations so that communities and relationships are more stable. The second factor is the protraction of pre and postnatal maturation. This can be seen as a solution to the obstetric problem posed by two apparently contradictory organic developments: on the one hand the human infant's enlarged brain and skull, and on the other the mother's narrower pelvic structure as a consequence of bipedalism. As a result infants need greater care and attention for a longer time. The tendency is already notable in primates whose young reach mental and physical maturity much more quickly than humans. The skull capacity of a human baby is about 25 per cent that of an adult, whereas the proportion is from 35 to 60 per cent in monkeys. However the relative immaturity of human infants is by no means an isolated biological phenomenon solely responsible for the institution of families and societies. The quantitative and qualitative development of the cerebral cortex, foetal immaturity and the human infant's prolonged dependence on adults are a series of related phenomena which should be seen as the consequences of a new mode of existence, specifically of hunting. In time the new-born human baby's immaturity turned out to be an advantage as well as a burden. Their plasticity makes them more readily responsive to neuro-muscular performances suggested or imposed by their educators. The child's earliest initiation into a general mode of existence and a specific environment might be compared to the acquisition of skills studied by ethologists (such as the organism's internalization of postures and movements). Training is superimposed on this at a later stage. We should not forget that until quite recently children were trained in practices and skills at a very tender age through observation, example and oral instruction alone. In this way the adult world with its tools and arts and its whole attitude to vegetation and animals was gradually impressed on their slowly maturing neuro-physiological system. Part of the innate ability to assimilate external elements and integrate them into existing behavioural patterns consists in developing available behaviour; such an ability surpasses genetic data, so that genetic reproduction is henceforth only partly responsible for natural human reproduction.

At the same time the relation between population and environment is inverted. After Malthus the general tendency to stress a population's dependence on available material resources increased. In technical terms population is defined as a dependent variable, fluctuating with the independent exogenous variable represented by resources. Darwinian biology made of this concept a law and applied it to all living creatures in an attempt to prove that whatever influences them genetically as regards growth and constitution expresses the organization and extent of their environment. Adaptation corresponds to a balance of quantity and quality achieved under such conditions which enables a population to survive and to multiply. That populations tend to remain constant in size is a theory we cannot discard offhand, but it can be (and has been) questioned. Thus C. Elton writes:

One of the most important generalizations that can be made about wild animal populations is that they fluctuate greatly in numbers. Naturalists of the nineteenth century took over without alteration the idea of the balance of life, i.e. constant populations. The earlier religious ideas had included the concept that the world was created in an orderly way, and disturbances in this order were attributed either to the acts of man himself or to the acts of God in punishing man for his presumption in upsetting this order, or perhaps in doing anything new at all. This general concept fitted naturally into the later biological theories of adaptation among animals, since it was supposed (rightly) that animals were closely adapted to their surroundings and (wrongly) that this adaptedness would lead to a state of steady balance between numbers of different species.[20]

Even if this assumption were correct it still does not explain what actually controls animal fertility. Variations in the size of animal populations have been attributed to variations in available food supplies, that is to the fertility and adequacy of the environment. But there is nothing to prove this, nor has the mechanism been discovered which would relate population growth exclusively to the quantity and quality of these supplies. Indeed a number of invalidating cases have come to light. For instance in Madagascar the lemur population does not consume all the food at its disposal; crabs decimated by the atomic explosion on the Eniwetok atoll later rebred there and reached their former density, feeding on the outer fibres of plants to compensate for the poor supply of algae. Such examples suggest that the members of a population tend to maintain a given population density, in spite of varied and variable food supplies. The idea of a hard and fast relation between population size and food supplies must be abandoned. D. H. Stott observes that: 'The popular Malthusian notion that the number surviving from year to year is dtermined by current supplies of food, with the excess dying from starvation, is no longer supported by any student of natural populations.'[21] However the basic stability within demographic fluctuations which this notion presupposes suggests that the pressure of 'superfluous' individuals in a population might have negative effects, such as the overexploitation of resources or the spread of infectious diseases, which would eliminate part of this population. The situation would then revert to normal, unless the species has been drastically reduced or has given birth to a different species because ecological barriers have interfered with gene circulation. This aspect is worthy of consideration, though it surely cannot apply to human beings, and perhaps not even to primates. Here population appears to constitute an independent variable, a positive factor in the control of the material world, and the demographic surplus plays a positive part by varying and improvising resources, activities and skills and through its migratory tendencies and superior adaptability to unfamiliar conditions.

The tendency for human communities to maintain a given density corresponding to the space and supplies at their disposal is a manifestation of the instinct of self-preservation and the urge to retain a delicate balance, which sooner or later will inevitably be lost. It is this loss of balance which is responsible for historical migrations and the discoveries and inventions which ultimately raise living standards. We have already discussed the phenomenon of overpopulation and its positive results in relation to hunting, and similar consequences have recently been observed in connection with agriculture.[22] Far from being a negative factor in evolution, disrupting a patiently established harmony, it plays a significant part in promoting new skills and a new relationship with the environment. It is an autonomous driving force rather than the outcome of totally extraneous environmental fluctuations. As usual Karl Marx was right when he said that the development of all productive forces is summarized in the development of population.[23] For the biological, physical and intellectual qualities of a species are as much part of its productive forces as is its technology.[24]

It is now obvious that the relation between organism and environment can no longer be seen as natural in the Darwinian sense, for the development of an important genetic and non-genetic reproductive potential and the tendency of populations to exceed their ecological boundaries reduce the pressure on genetic mutations to a mere virtuality. Moreover when certain groups of an animal community are obliged to leave their natural habitat (to migrate, for instance, from prairie to desert) or when this habitat undergoes a climatic upheaval (which reduces the prairie to desert, for instance) they are submitted to sudden variations of climate and vegetation. Such geographical discontinuity obviously affects individual mortality and genotypes and transforms specific hereditary or acquired qualities. On the other hand when a sub-group has reached the evolutionary stage with which we are concerned here, it is conditioned by social mechanisms such as hierarchy to adopt unfamiliar, unexploited resources, and to create a whole new mode of life without having to give up the old and break irrevocably with the past. Such was the case with predacity. Furthermore the transition which occurred in human and proto-hominid sub-groups was mediated by another sub-group; the hunters migrated from the forest to the marshlands after they had already assimilated biopsychic anthropoid or hominid predatory behaviour. Man's relation to reality is forever established through another man's having previously assimilated some of its aspects, albeit temporarily, into his physical and mental make-up. The role of natural selection could almost be said to end here.

Fundamental processes often establish their own frontiers where they merge with a different process — as solar systems, obeying their own laws, explode, become extinct or enter the orbit of another system. Universality and permanence are hard to attain and harder to maintain. 20 or perhaps 40 million years ago normal selection contributed to the emerging of a new pattern of relationships between organisms and environment. Just as natural selection was the result of a transition so it made possible the transition to a new beginning – that is, to the birth of an unprecedented activity of objective forces within the material world. Becoming autonomous, this activity provoked a simultaneous schism within a species of anthropoid gatherers, and man the hunter emerged. The divisions between male and female and between animal and plant resources are a result of this activity. 'In contrast to carnivora,' say Washburn and Lancaster, 'human hunting, if done by males, is based on a division of labour and is a social and technical adaptation quite different from that of other mammals.' [25]

The observation is pertinent, but an essential point should be stressed. The division indicates a separation of the material world, in relation to the species' various spheres of activity, abilities and aptitudes. It is not a mere specialization of tasks, a sub-division or division of labour. The specialization of activities and purposes improves skill, social organization and productivity, but it does not imply a series of different relationships with the natural world. Sub-division within a specific activity such as hunting, gathering, cultivating or craftsmanship is one thing and the division between these activities is quite another. The former is a specialization of general skills and methods; the latter involves the creation of different and often contradictory skills and methods. With the appearance of man this division provided a new solution to a problem hitherto solved by natural selection: the problem of reproducing the species and adapting it to the environment. I have described how this solution operated in the particular case of hunting, and elsewhere I have shown[26] that it is a common factor in the emergence of qualities which distinguish a portion of humanity, and in the translation of these qualities to another portion, while relations between humanity and the environment are inverted. The conditions for such inversion of population components and biological and physical potentialities are firstly a state of imbalance in these components; and secondly the coincidence of auxiliary resources (food, tools and skills) with a group of supernumerary individuals. Such a coincidence realizes and connects the potential properties of both terms. Thus in every age a human category emerges – for example, hunters, cultivators, craftsmen – endowed with the skills, biological qualities and practical abilities capable of creating a secondary relationship between organism and environment which finally replaces the old. The contrast between each category involves a redefinition of the elements and their reorganization within a changed environment. In the forest vegetation provided shelter and subsistence for early communities for whom stones were obstacles to be removed or avoided. When predacity began the forest was still a shelter, but stones were turned into weapons and tools. The contrast has a further significance, reflected in human and in non-human relationships, in the relationship between hunter and cultivator and between the animal and the vegetable world. Thus the division created within humanity has its counterpart in the universe.

2 *The Role of Man and the Role of Woman*

(a) *Invention and growth*

From a purely realistic point of view invention is an ordinary phenomenon. It can be detected in the urge to explore, to solve minor or major problems and to combine operations or substances for a given purpose. Inspiration, chance and personal genius may assist invention, but they are not indispensable. Invention is the ability to use skills, information or reflexes in unprecedented ways, so that they emerge as new skills, information or reflexes. This involves the simultaneous reorganization and substitution of physical and biological resources, and the appearance of previously unknown effects. Human and non-human qualities and elements evolve side by side in a shared universe. The animal caught in a snare is no less an invention than the wooden tool fashioned with a piece of flint or the act of standing upright to handle a missile. What we call arts and resources are created in this way, and they reflect the broadening and combining of modes and spheres of existence. Specialization indicates the evolution of the relation between population and environment, for it opens new possibilities in a stable, predetermined structure, where all the elements appear to fit together perfectly. A foraging primate or hominid population is dependent on a particular type of vegetation; its habitat is limited to a given area wherein it performs a specific function; its behaviour patterns and its sensory and mental apparatus correspond to the kind of stimuli it receives and to the spatial distribution peculiar to the inanimate objects that circumscribe and people its world. What is created in this way is a 'man-matter system' (fauna and flora being part of the matter), patiently built up, which can be defined, described and analysed. For a long time the system can continue its effective, independent existence. But as the importance of predacity increases the system becomes extended and enriched. Foraging habits and activities are transferred to scavenging and then to trapping, and territorial frontiers are extended to include hunting grounds.

At a given stage evolution takes a different course and faithful reproduction gives way to inventiveness. Activities become diversified, while each of them is generally considered indispensable to the survival of the community. The long sequence of substitutions begins. As good hunting grounds rather than abundant vegetation dictate the choice of camping sites, the forest home is abandoned for the marshland cave. Human ingenuity was responsible for this innovation, and for others no less surprising, of which the most significant consequence was undoubtedly the diversification of customs, activities and ecological niches. Thus a new 'man-matter system' diverges from the old and the species is now able to subsist in two distinct habitats corresponding to two natural relationships. What has in fact taken place is the division of a single habitat. Biosocial unity has bridged the gap between separate territories by both sub-dividing and superposing space so that hunting and gathering areas are distinct yet congruous. However the pressures of a centrifugal impulse to explore and a centripetal urge to preserve familiar, localized resources alternate, and are responsible for the present state of much of our flora and fauna. They diversify and extend the environment as befits a larger or more demanding population. One way of solving the problem of overpopulation is for distinct hunting and gathering communities to disperse over vaster areas. But the problem is more satisfactorily solved if these dispersed communities combine both activities. Moreover the risk of speciation is eliminated, not so much because human beings now live in diversified geological, climatic and alimentary conditions, as because they modify the environment where such conditions prevail. Ecology takes over from genetics as a diversified biosphere reduces the need for organic selectivity.

This largely explains the change which took place about 500,000 years ago. First various species of hominid coexisted as do so many other species. Then migrations and geomorphological barriers biologically diversified them. After the evolutionary phenomenon of *Homo erectus* humanity was represented by a single species, or a single Mendelian population with a common genetic constitution. Hunting and the inventions it involved had already perfected the art of creating various environments for one species, and it was no longer necessary to provide various species for one environment. Diversified conditions had encouraged genetic mutations which, owing to the uniformity of the species, spread rapidly to constitute the elements of the human genotype.

During this period organic mutations and the emergence of new skills and resources were the immediate result of recurrent overpopulation problems. Later, populations in search of a world they could call their own, where they could settle and thrive, deliberately created such problems; for them 'more' was no longer 'too many'. But whether the subsequent divisions of the species were due to accidental or to deliberate demographic imbalance, inventiveness certainly improved with each of these divisions. It corresponds to a population's urge to expand and to acquire the skills which can satisfy this urge. More important than numerical growth itself are the readjustments such growth entails. The addition of hunting to gathering does not simply mean that five thousand can now feed where only a thousand subsisted formerly. These five thousand must possess different faculties and be capable of putting them to the best possible use in the pursuit of specific tasks. Each biological or non-biological character is identified with the corresponding activity for as long as this is necessary. This account might appear to contradict the theory of the survival of the fittest, since here it is the underprivileged individuals whom evolution has favoured. But survival is not concerned with individuals, but with the species. Natural division enables a species to acquire new characteristics and thus to survive in altered circumstances thanks to the spirit of inventiveness. Invention is not the discovery of something new, but only of new ways of using what already exists and of making it available to all. Invention benefits the community and its main purpose is public recognition.

(b) Transmitting and preserving

A biological species is reproduced by means of mutations and selective adaptations. Individuals are born with the required characteristics and mature rapidly. Population size and functional divisions are mainly controlled by genetic processes that maintain procreation and specialization at an optimum level. Should these processes fail individual survival is wholly determined by the environment. In some of the more advanced animal societies social structure is preserved through the transmission from generation to generation of established customs. As far as we know the higher primates were the first to have escaped complete genetic determinism by transmitting and moulding the biopsychological qualities required by their social organization. Thus social reproduction fulfils a specific function while diverging from natural reproduction. The latter mediates between the species and the environment so that specific qualities recur with undiminished efficiency. The species is preserved through — not in — the individual whose natural aptitudes and reactions are stimulated. Natural reproduction in all animal species, perhaps even in the higher primates, is mainly genetic. With the emergence of hominids natural reproduction became an autonomous, purposeful process. This modification was due to a longer life-span as well as to the new-born infant's slower maturation. But these factors cannot account for the reproduction of distinct human categories, that is of differentiated reproduction. The individuals of a given species are generally included in a single system of relationships and activities, even when their functions are specialized; whereas the members of human populations are divided into widely differentiated sectors within distinct or even contradictory systems of relationships and activities. Such a differentiation was inevitable, in view of the conditions in which abilities are practised and produced and resources exploited. For the organization of particular abilities and their relation to the human organism precludes the practice of activities requiring incompatible aptitudes by a single group of individuals. Whereas a hunter lies in wait, stalks, pursues or captures an animal for the sole purpose of putting it to death, a shepherd fattens and tends his flock, maintaining it in the best possible condition until it is required. An engineer improves his skill and knowledge, overcomes one obstacle after another with the help of instruments and inventions, while an artisan attains his ends by the exercise of manual dexterity, coordinating his gestures and becoming familiar with the qualities of his material. Each speciality requires the reproduction of particular abilities to preserve and perfect a range of specific qualities. The organic elements peculiar to each intellectual or physical activity induce those who practise it to avoid other activities which might hinder the development of such elements.

The division between gatherers and hunters is subject to similar restrictions. Wherever it occurs individuals are preconditioned to their allotted activity almost from birth, either through initiation or, in the case of primates and hominids, by simple familiarization. Moreover their very right to exist must be justified. Infanticide may or may not be a common practice, but it certainly represents the most efficient method of selective reproduction. There is undisputed evidence that not only in Pleistocene societies, but even in some Australian and Eskimo communities today between 15 and 50 per cent of infants who are born are systematically destroyed. Since these are hunting communities, the victims, needless to say, are girls whereas in primate societies the 'supernumerary' potential are males.

For a very long time gathering and hunting continued to be practised according to prehominid methods, so that the training of those children who were allowed to live was unsophisticated to say the least. It began by a process of sensory and kinetic adaptation to the environment which would not extend beyond the age of biological maturity. Girls would hardly require any special training to become proficient gatherers. Boys, on the other hand, have to be instructed in tracking and snaring tactics, taught to distinguish the individual cries and smells of various animals, and trained to control their gestures and synchronize them with those of their future partners. Advice, topography and directions are stored in their collective and individual memory while reflexes are atuned to weapons, tools and substances. Appropriate exercises must be performed to develop and strengthen the whole organism, but certain relevant muscles receive particular attention. Tribes hunting in kayaks submit their youths to special muscle-stretching exercises as soon as they are able to walk. The boy is made to sit on a level surface with his legs extended in front of him, while his father or another male member of the family stands behind him and pulls his throwing arm up and back as far as it will go. This exercise is generally accompanied by rhythmic chants which will fix it in the lad's memory. By the time he is fully grown the flexibility of his shoulder-joint is such that he can throw javelin or harpoon with considerable force and precision while seated in his kayak. Further exercises consist of pushing the seated boy forward to strengthen his back muscles, or repeatedly flexing his knees to prevent the rigidity which would naturally result from the prolonged immobility such forms of hunting require. Similar more or less complicated exercises are the rule in most hunting populations. Their regular enforcement establishes the rhythm of a boy's childhood and literally shapes his anatomy, marking the various stages of his journey towards manhood.

The transmission of physical and intellectual skills is more than just teaching and learning and thus procuring the replacement of individuals and groups. It also ensures the reproduction of a specific relationship to the environment. This environment is the place where objects and supplies can be found. But it is also a book written by successive generations, recording the migrations of populations, their influence on the distribution of animals and plants, and the way in which climate, watercourses and mountains have determined the choice of routes or settlements. It must be deciphered and internalized by the children of the species, together with the ancestral divisions of night and day and the seasons of the year, with their related activities.

Reproducing individuals thus involves reproducing the environment, for when a given aptitude is lost the corresponding features of the environment vanish as well. When men cease to hunt a species of game or cease to hunt altogether, the distribution of animal populations and the whole framework of living space with its internal interactions are affected; when something is ignored it gradually loses its objective and subjective reality. The energy which preserves and renews such activities is materialized in the population's wealth, achievements and growth, and this same energy preserves and renews a population's environment and its social structure. But it also creates the divisions between human beings. For the reproduction of specialized individuals perpetuates distinctions between categories — male and female, hunters and gatherers — each category being related to its own material world with which it forms a coherent, distinct system. Individuals are maintained and trained not as members of a species, but as members of a 'natural category', that is a group of beings who, despite their biological and social similarity to the rest of the community, possess distinct intellectual and physical abilities and a distinct symbiosis with the environment. Every time men create and exploit internal or external resources they do so as representatives of a given category, and are thus estranged from one another to the exact extent that their respective categories are distinct.

We must then conclude that this reproduction is natural. It assists and extends biological evolution, or the retention of mutations which facilitate the species' adaptation to its environment. It has a regular function which is to consolidate the relationship between a population and its natural surroundings. On the other hand it differentiates the ever-increasing flow of living human substance in order to adapt it to the ecological configurations it has created. Obviously such an adaptation is a reaction to man-made and not to natural configurations. Thus through his influence on the environment man establishes a new interdependence between its elements, parallel to the interdependence between natural categories, or biological and geomorphological factors. Animate and inanimate objects participate in the history of man after participating in his evolution.

3 *Sub-division as a Natural Phenomenon*

This theory has the advantage of accounting for most zoological and prehistorical problems, especially the all-important question of cynegetization. It explains the generality of social factors in organic evolution and their influence on genetic processes; the use of improvised tools by various animal species, and the intermittent nature of such occurrences; and the fact that predatory skills antedate the physical and anatomical transformation of man. It is more constructive to consider society as a dynamic complex rather than to concentrate on the psychological and physiological characteristics of individual members of a species. Moreover the parallels between primate and human customs and behaviour make it difficult to gauge their significance independently. Correspondences and contrasts can only be related to a sequence which, though not necessarily uninterrupted, nor composed of strictly interdependent elements, must be seen as a whole if we are to distinguish its more relevant stages. This does not imply that we shall finally be in a position to piece togther a regular pattern of evolution. Evolution made a number of false starts and followed highly divergent tracks at one time or another. Yet by and large the process has been substantially uniform.

Even if our theory arouses no overt objections it cannot fail to shock, for it posits division as a natural phenomenon in the history of mankind. It is generally presumed that organic evolution and natural selection suddenly cease to operate when social evolution took over: in other words that huminization was provisionally victorious at a given stage in the universal battle for survival. Such a simplification is not very helpful since it ignores the process of our own evolution and the circumstances which made it possible and inevitable. Moreover as a theory it is no longer empirically justified. E. W. Caspari writes:

It has sometimes been maintained that in the evolution of man adaptation by cultural means has taken the place of adaptation by genetic means. This implies that the morphological and biological evolution of man took place first and that cultural evolution has taken over afterward. Our present knowledge seems to contradict this assumption since it is known that our human ancestors already possessed a certain degree of culture, as evidenced by tool making, before they had reached all the morphological characteristics of modern man, particularly modern brain size. Our present considerations show that the process must have been more complicated. As soon as cultural activities had started, they must have had a feedback on the biological activities of man, since the existence of culture would change the adaptive value of genes considerably.[27]

To say that human social factors have influenced an eminently natural historical progression is no longer a paradox. Though the respective influences on animals and men of genetics and society are different, there is no reason to assume that the first are natural and the second not. At most they are natural in different ways, the first being concerned with selection and adaptation, the second with division and growth. We have explained the reasons for the substitution of one for the other and the circumstances which brought it about. The metamorphosis and restructuring of human and non-human resources can always be traced back to a natural division, and they are always experienced as natural. Again and again the obstacles that restricted innovation or opposition are overcome and new organic or inorganic possibilities are realized. Agriculture and hunting are different from gathering not so much in their purpose as in their attitude to this purpose, and in the more or less protracted period of initiation and apprenticeship they require. Whenever one such complex of skills emerges those which preceded it become outdated or disappear. As a result man's relation to the environment is altered, as well as the constitution and growth of the species. Skills, wealth and energy obviously accumulate and gradually increase the sum total of what has been invented or reproduced over the centuries. But one system of phenomena, objects and beings invariably predominates, not simply as the principal, basic resource, but as the general motivating power. Nature has been moulded in succession by animals and the hunter, neuro-muscular aptitudes and the craftsman, mechanical energy and the mechanic. The cycle which includes these zoomorphic, organic or mechanical states, each of which was for its contemporaries final, records the creation and hierarchy of natural divisions of the universe, as distinct human categories capable of establishing them emerge; that is to say as specific skills and aptitudes happen to coincide with circumstances favouring the reorganization of material potentials.

The constantly renewed realtionship between man and his environment is a two-way exchange. The striding foot, the watchful eye and the prehensile hand, besides being related to specific activities and skills, are part of a general material and ecological structure. The hunter's instincts are quickened by his prey; techniques develop the neuro-muscular apparatus; man and his environment constitute a single complex in the sequence of life-cycles of the biosphere in which he is one of the organizing factors. Through the differentiation of his aptitudes man recreates himself both genetically and naturally. But it is surely premature to infer that the age of anatomical and physiological modifications is ended, that only the superstructure of acquired artefacts and knowledge continues to change. How can we foresee what significance imperceptible biological transformations may not acquire some day. Furthermore modern man, the latest representative of a species, is, relatively speaking, barely half way round the track. Physical forces have become part of his nature, but the same was true for his forefathers. The human body is a book in which the laws of cosmic elements are inscribed. Man's senses, organs, muscles and brain can reproduce the natural forces and simultaneously contain their essence, the laws and principles which convert such forces into part of himself. Skills and tools, the social coordination of activities and procreation combine to integrate the material environment into his constitution and, conversely, to adapt his constitution to the environment. This was made possible by the recurring sub-divisions of the species, which had a decisive impact on its speciation and on the emergence of most of its biological characteristics. Such characteristics are no more artificial than those of primates or sharks, or the mutations which have occurred in a number of animals or plants as a result of man's appearance on earth.

Man's interventions in organic evolutionary phenomena, like his interventions in chemical and physical phenomena, do not make division more artificial than selection; they are both natural in the same way. T. Dobzhansky writes: 'Natural' in "natural selection" does not mean the state of affairs preceding or excluding man-made changes.'[28] By accepting such a notion we avoid the paradox of recognizing man's place in nature as a genetic, organic being and excluding him from nature on account of his individual and social achievements. Moreover we acknowledge the fact that he participates in a progression that leads inevitably to a natural order, not to a humanized nature. Such a nature could only be superficially cultivated, remaining fundamentally unchanged, by the intervention of an eternally extraneous agent. Yet the act of transforming is creative; it produces a specific historical organization of reality and of human faculties. It is impossible to find a criterion which would enable us to see man as natural in one sense and unnatural in another. The process by which man became man is part of his own history.

Part Three

Animal Societies and Human Societies

[VI]

Did Human Society Spring from Chaos?

1 *Society Versus Nature*

A radical change is taking place. Our concepts of individuality and of instinct are no longer what they were. When we say 'society' today we mean animal as well as human collectivities. Even the environment we have created is gradually coming to be seen as natural. Parts One and Two of this work stress this fusion of social with natural reality, and also refer to the significance of our new scientific approach to the relationship between man and nature. Part Three deals with its social implications, more particularly in relation to primitive human societies and their genesis.

All traditional theories and definitions of society conform more or less faithfully to a pattern which is based on three things. (a) A formula: Society is a departure from nature. *(b)* A question: How does society overcome nature's intrinsic chaos? And *(c)* a definition: Society is a secondary reality. Society and nature are discontinuous and it is retrogressive and dangerous to try and link them together. Social organization has nothing to do with the organic or inorganic world. Men are socially organized beings, entrenched in a biosphere they exploit and dominate by artificial means. They have neither the opportunity nor the desire to condition or influence it fundamentally. With the help of further artefacts they control their own instincts and passions. They have mastered the world and themselves and they are wholly exceptional beings.

The passage from the highest form of animal life to the most elementary form of human life acquires an aura of sanctity. Our original state had a kind of transparency; the raw material which we have been fashioning ever since was then directly perceptible. So we try to discern the essence of sociability and thus the basis of subsequent social institutions in these remote and difficult beginnings. Reconstructions of primate and early human communities for such comparative or analytical purposes postulate two complementary premises. Firstly the characteristics of the community are those of the organisms which compose it. Secondly society is an unstable grouping of individuals. According to the first, animal societies, unlike biological organisms, are unspecific; according to the second, they are unlike human societies in that they are biological. In this way the course of evolution is readily traced. In the beginning inner nature was the *individual*, the constitutive psycho-biological unit, and what mattered were the instincts and inherited powers of the individual. External nature was then the totality of the material environment. Then man, responding to intrinsic, independent motivations, as a strictly predetermined, autonomous product of evolution, was able to adapt more or less successfully to the environment into which he emerged. He might, in his relative autonomy, have done without society altogether, were it not for the innate imperfections of the race and the requirements of procreation.

According to this thesis, the irreducible core of all behaviour, which is spontaneous and predictable, is natural instinct or the hereditary genetic equipment. In animals all behaviour is like this. Children and savages – especially where sexual and aggressive urges are concerned – also show little concern for others or for the interests of society. Thus among all animals, including primates, promiscuity and anarchy are the law. In man, though such tendencies are under control, they correspond to his inner nature.

Society, on the other hand, is seen as a derived, and not a natural system. It is an acquired system which combines distinct individuals into families, classes or regional collectivities possessing laws, religions and rights. Its function might be compared to that of a language which, by superimposing syntax on sound phenomena, turns them into mutually dependent words and sentences to convey messages. Furthermore society restrains natural individual impulses so that they conform to collective interests. Renunciation and constraint are man's weapons, and kinship was the first fortress he erected in the battle he wages against his animal nature. Without such defences all men would be like the barbaric tribes described by Euripides' Hermione: 'Father with daughter, son with mother weds, Sister with brother: kin the nearest wade through blood: their laws forbid no whit thereof' [1] Such conditions are obviously not conducive to cooperation and unselfish relationships; they create conflicts and rivalry, threaten stability, continuity and individual survival. It is for this reason that laws were introduced.

Unfortunately all manifestations of culture, such as kinship, values, education, art and science are only an outer crust beneath which passion rumbles, ever ready to erupt in 'a confusion of generations, an unbridling of instincts and a violent reversal of convention', as Malinowski prophesies.[2] Society was founded to forestall such catastrophes. It represents the curbing of a natural spontaneity which preceded and still underlies it, of irrational tendencies which are the ineradicable remnants of primitive nature. Repression is the form adaptation assumes in human evolution.

According to the second premise the emergence of society marks the beginning of a new order which turned the unstable associations of biological groups into consistent, specifically human social relationships. Prehuman groups responded to hormonic cycles; matings were fortuitious, reciprocal relations unpredictable;[3] distinctions between age and youth or kin and non-kin were non-existent. Then man came on the scene to distinguish between good and evil and between himself and others; to prescribe, in other words, the laws of marriage, production and communication. Like Maxwell's demon he established frontiers where none existed and turned the course of history which was heading straight for chaos. It will be remembered that the famous physicist Maxwell imagined a demon controlling the passage of a gas from one container to another at an identical temperature. By operating an imaginary sluice he can effortlessly assist or impede the circulation of molecules between containers; more precisely, he can allow the flow of slow, weak molecules in one direction while the fast, strong molecules flow in the other. After a certain time one of the containers will become heated and the other cold without loss or transformation of energy. Matrimonial, economic and linguistic social systems have had similar 'demonic' results. The existence of each separate being follows a predetermined course, merging harmoniously with the others, and each biological group has its own particular place in a system of alliances. Moderation replaces excess and the good of the community that of the individual. The boundary between culture and nature is the historical outcome of a process of a selection.

According to this theory society sprang fully fledged from its exact opposite – chaotic, organic, individualistic bestiality – after a period of transition represented by 'natural' primitive collectivities. Primitivism, as concept and reality, stands for the birth of our basic, specific distinctness, for it implies a break rather than a genesis, or the accidental creation of something from nothing, rather than the gradual development of the conditions for human communality. Human culture then progresses inexplicably from the prehuman, becoming increasingly principled and complex and, of course, less natural and spontaneous. Such an extraordinary phenomenon can only have an extraordinary purpose. Society was born to overcome bestiality and maintain it for ever under control. This it achieves by preserving its independence from its individual members whom it disciplines. Our basic unruliness and promiscuity, as well as the lack of natural resources, the threat of overpopulation and the adversity of the elements, required and still require a steadfast, concerted resistance. Had a general state of harmony predominated from the start we would not have had to create society, which is none other than the solution of a universal problem that no other species could solve. Thus the phenomenon we had to explain, the singular evolution of mankind, becomes its own explanation. For all living creatures except man society is a *secondary* reality; but even for man it is an acquired reality.

2 *Order and Disorder*

Alone or in groups animals are always subject to biological vicissitudes. But though men suffer the constrictions of the environment and the ascendancy of heredity as individuals, once they are grouped together they form a society.

A basic duality characterizes the human species. We subsist simultaneously on two contradictory levels: the innate personal and the acquired social. 'There are, therefore, two major categories of facts,' says Claude Levi-Strauss. 'One links us to the animal kingdom by virtue of everything we are, because of our birth and the characteristics which have been passed down to us by our parents and ancestors, these characteristics being of a biological, and sometimes of a psychological, nature; the other consists of the whole artificial universe which we live in as members of a community.'[4]

All that pertains to this 'artificial world', all that we see as altogether superior — rationality, science, art, civilization, symbolic communication — is a means of suppressing imperious desires or a general, autonomous, organic process. Moreover we are implicitly invited to collaborate in this suppression, if we do not want to relapse into prehistoric chaos and forego the support of a collective, organized system. This is roughly how most of our institutions vindicate their existence and it is what is implied in our biological and sociological theories. It also dominates our everyday existence.

Yet we cannot help wondering if this obsession with human order as opposed to animal disorder, this aversion to all that is spontaneous, organic and instinctive, has not distorted our vision of the world and of ourselves. The astounding platitudes we hear about animal or primitive societies where 'natural' instinct is the only law, are credible only because of the mutual complicity of tellers and audiences. When certain tendencies are not restrained there is no denying that they may provoke conflicts and dissipation, but these consequences are by no means inevitable. In many communities fathers, sons and brothers happily share one female, or mothers, daughters and sisters one male. Incest is not condemned everywhere even in human societies. Where it occurs it is accepted by all concerned without any sign of antagonism. When conflicts do arise they are easily controlled, as the relatively common practice of polygamy and polyandry testifies. It is quite wrong to imagine that human society created harmony in the place of a natural, fundamentally disorganized or distorted mode of existence; or that it effectively repressed the passions which preclude peaceful coexistence in all the other species. We would do well to remember that, if the virtues civilization has neglected to preach are few and far between, the crimes it has successfully avoided are even fewer. If law, prohibition, the family and hierarchy were really conceived to eliminate the destructive violence of organic passion that dominates other species, then, to judge by the result, they have sadly failed in their purpose. The conditions of collective coexistence described by the zoologist are ideal compared to those reported by historians – or even to those which an average human being who has reached maturity in the middle of the present century can see for himself.

However our accumulated experience, a greater insight into our fears and prejudices and into the apparent pointlessness of this continued struggle against our basic nature tend to encourage a more enlightened perspective. A number of conventional theories are being questioned. Two, in particular, can be discarded straight away. *(a)* The notion of the individual as the irreducible basic unit of analysis inevitably recalls the mechanistic theory of the unsplittable atom as the basic unit from which all matter is constituted and in which all the properties of matter are to be found. Here the individual is seen as bearing the principles of heredity and custom, and his contact with the environment is unmediated. Moreover the struggle for survival usually favours the fittest. Thus each being represents the whole species and constitutes a complete biological unit. Complex, or social, structures are compounds of simple elements each of which retains its distinct identity – like a pure chemical substance when combined with others. This theory has suffered the same fate as that of the unsplittable atom. We know that individuals represent transitional conformations which can transmit the hereditary principles they carry in their chromosomes and which mutate independently. Cell metabolism and reproduction obey a code which is inscribed in the nucleic acids of the basic double helix and communicated through chemical messages. The agents determining organic attributes, births and deaths, are as accurately programmed as possible; they are preadjusted to repeat themselves indefinitely. They combine to reproduce the regular structure of the species, not of the single individual. The latter is inscribed on the genetic grid as one of the many possible versions which might have come into being, given the right conditions. From an evolutionary point of view he is a member of a population whose organisms are not identical specimens of an iterative sequence but instead present a multitude of variations. The population is distinguished by the range of such variations, and an isolated individual or type will never be more than partly representative of the whole. Even at the biological level aggregate and individual are mutually inclusive.

This new approach also invalidates the belief that an individual deprived of human contact reverts inevitably to bestiality. The idea that animals cannot live socially because they are governed by the blind, purposeless forces which constitute natural instinct may be a convenient theory but it is entirely unfounded. Only the domestic animal lives exclusively for himself; the biological animal is more circumspect. Instinctive behaviour is autonomous in that it involves uniformity, autonomy and a certain predictability.[5] But the conventions and rituals of animal sexual and aggressive interactions cannot be ignored by anyone who takes the study of animal behaviour seriously. For instance, incitement and response behaviour conforms to specific conventions which have nothing to do with the animal's physical and anatomical structure nor with the environment. Dogs wag their tails as a sign of friendliness, whereas cats wag theirs in anger. The connection between the innate capacity of a species to execute a signal and the purpose of such a signal is arbitrary. The relation between tail-wagging and friendliness or anger could be reversed and the purpose would be unchanged. The meaning of a given gesture as encouragement or warning is based on convention and on nothing else. In a number of species fighting is strictly ritualistic and reflects hierarchy. Codes of behaviour are both hereditary and acquired by initiation and imitation, but they are collectively observed. Virulence is controlled by appropriate devices. It has been noted that members of certain species usually avoid direct confrontation if they can, though this tendency may disappear in captivity. A wild male feline marks out his territory by leaving a trail of smell so that other members of the species will know its boundaries and refrain from crossing them. Hierarchy minimizes the risk of conflict in most affiliation societies where strictly observed priorities eliminate, or at least greatly reduce, the possibility of discord. If a quarrel does occur it never goes very far. The weaker party usually resorts either to flight or to expressions of submission which entail exposing the more vulnerable parts of his anatomy to his adversary.

Sexual relations conform to similar patterns. Coupling and fighting are carefully ritualized to ensure survival or satisfaction. Instinctive behaviour is not passive; it consolidates intra-specific relations and revives them as circumstances require. Far from disrupting animal societies such behaviour patterns promote solidarity and sociability, stimulating spatial and temporal coexistence. Subordinates seek the protection of their superiors, aggressors are merciful to their victims, and sexual parades attract partners who are predetermined by social or physiological conventions. Nature is not necessarily disruptive or antisocial. Society and natural instincts are by no means incompatible. The social individual remains as biological, or as biologically unadulterated, as the isolated individual. Animals in captivity show signs of unresolved behaviour because their inner reactions are weaker or have lost their biological significance. As for man and those species which most resemble him, they are less 'natural' alone than with their kind. Anthropological and psychological hypotheses concerning 'wolf children' – young children who, having been deprived of contact with civilized adults, revert to animal behaviour – are heuristically invalid. In other words any individual living in total isolation will necessarily be unrepresentative of the species, because he will be neurologically, physiologically and psychologically deficient. Our sensory, instinctive and intellectual apparatus, as with all relatively developed mammals, are epigenetically predisposed and constituted for interdependence, the development of communicative abilities and specifically social activities. Of course there is no way of observing the normal, independent development in animals or children of impulses or faculties which might, strictly speaking, be called individual, and of comparing such a development with one that might be defined as social. However the organic properties of living creatures in natural conditions are stimulated rather than atrophied or distorted by association with their like. It is quite pointless and unrealistic to see coordinated, controlled behaviour as unnatural. In fact collective interactions and biological phenomena converge and are mutually influential. They replace and relay each other to achieve a common end.

In the animal world natural spontaneous actions are frequently ritualized to become symbolic attitudes of parade and exhibition. Such 'rites' are as important as the act itself. They express the power and restraint of impulses peculiar to a species, its capacity for self-motivation and retrospection and, through deliberate attitudinizing, the individual's unambiguous awareness of others. Indeed a lack of such awareness is a symptom of pathological rather than natural conditions. The problem of reconciling spontaneity and convention is the same in animal as in human societies, and each solves it after its own fashion. If our social conventions were lost or forgotten we would not lapse into a state of non-social lawlessness; we would find new models of social behaviour in the animal world. Our own social organizations are not the only means of keeping primitive innate instincts at bay; animal societies provide the necessary restraint for animal instincts. As Konrad Lorenz observes, the evolution of instinctive behaviour in the zoological system proves how pointless it is to speak of 'instinct', for our observations are limited to innate reactions, or the instinctive *behaviour* of a restricted portion of this system.[6]

For one reason or another, we are becoming gradually less convinced of the aptness of such hard and fast divisions of reality[7] into two distinct and contradictory compartments, the biological and the social. We now see that the social is not an extraneous addition artificially superimposed on the biological. The organic, fully developed being does not precede the specific population of which he is a member. Individual and society are linked in a common process of organization and evolution.

(b) Another outdated assumption is that human society and nature suddenly parted company so that their history is one of increasing

estrangement. This posed three questions. How did social order spring from its contrary, that is from nature? What are their respective characteristics? And what provoked the presumed discrepancy between them? To answer these questions the non-social world must be seen as totally lacking in stability and order.

At one time the savage appeared to mark the frontier between the two states. For Hegel he was a 'natural, unrestrained' being, knowing neither 'God nor Law'. Culture — the family, religion, education and rationality — only existed on one side of the frontier. Then the travellers' tales and philosophical speculations were confounded by anthropological revelations, and it became evident that these savages were, in fact, eminently social beings who were not ignorant of the priorities of age and sex, xenophobia, infanticide, cooperation, trade, superstitions, or the prohibition of basic pleasures. As Freud observed no one would expect the sexual life of these poor naked cannibals to be normal in the usual sense of the term, and their sexual urges submitted to any form of restraint. Yet in fact they are very careful and scrupulous in avoiding all incestuous relationship.'[8] So the barrier had to be moved to exclude only non-human species. The attributes of non-sociability remained unchanged, but the concepts of individuality and instinct were revised. Ethologists, following the example of anthropologists, set off to observe 'savage' populations on the spot, and reported that they could find no evidence at all of the bestial promiscuity, purely biological associations and presocial or antisocial conditions they had expected. Now we know that primates possess a definite social structure; that their sexual life, systems of communication and so on reflect a given order and permanent norms which, though different from our own, are nonetheless collectively acknowledged and carefully transmitted. Indeed promiscuity appears to be an exclusively human problem, which rarely or never arises in simian societies where its presence denotes a state of social breakdown.

However although the truth of such revelations is not questioned, their impact is generally minimized. Thus F. R. Service writes: 'A "natural" biological group is amorphous apart from priority, sexual partnerships (where they exist) and the mother-child dyad.' [9] But may we ask on what basis it is said to be amorphous, and at what stage do priorities and stable relationships become social? Indeed these communities can only be disqualified *a priori* in order to preserve the illusion of human distinctness. For a purely organic, instinctual 'horde' cannot be found among primates any more than it can or ever could be found among human beings. As Washburn and Jay say:

> It is hard to imagine a more striking contrast than that between the present concept of an organised society, largely based on social activities, affectively or cooperatively motivated, and the former notion

of an undisciplined band of monkeys ruled by a despot. The nineteenth-century champions of evolution saw primitive communities as far less organised than are, in fact, simian and anthropoid societies today.[10]

The new frontier turns out to be neither more impregnable nor better placed than the old. Of course human and primate societies differ in a great many obvious ways, such as individual characteristics, the predominance of innate over acquired qualities and relationship with the environment. Over the centuries Maxwell's 'demon' patiently contrived these divergences. But he did so by modifying the coordinates of a process generating equivalent organizations, and not by regulating the flow of isolated biological molecules. However much we may wish to distinguish culture and nature, to present nature as long since superseded by society, or as the opposite of society, we will always come up against a more remote but still undeniably social animal or primitive structure.

Society is an original, positive reality, like matter or life. It has a specific economy which stems from that of nature with which it is integrated. It has been created and recreated by many species in succession, and its permanence lies in its peculiar ability to change with changing circumstances. It is no more the product of makeshift solutions to extraneous malfunctions than biological systems are the product of physico-chemical anomalies. Circumstances which were partly accidental made desirable some form of social coexistence which, as survival became more and more problematic, underwent various adaptations and merged with a number of objective processes. Society is a fundamental, organic option similar to bilateral symmetry or sexual reproduction.[11] Its positive role in evolution makes the notion of a strictly biological evolution unrealistic. Man did not invent society but simply gave it a particular structure.

It is time we realized that not only man, but his social structure as well, 'descended' from the ape. The continuity is evident biologically and materially. Human societies are based on 'conventions'; but so too are many animal collectivities in their relation to the environment, which tends after a time to become standardized and inevitable. Socialized events and activities condition other events and activities and become part of a continuous system of reactions. The priorities of sex and age evolve into status distinctions and recur on every behavioural chart right up to the present. At every stage a new internal coherence is established and a new congruence with the environment is developed. In such a sequence it is impossible to assert that one society is 'more' a society than another. Some may be better or more satisfactory than others, but we are not concerned with classifications. Moreover since all societies are equally social as regards their purpose, structure and adaptedness to circumstances, there is no reason why we should not study the evolution of our own from its first emergence as a substitute for primate societies of affiliation which in fact are part of its history.

Once we have accepted this fact, our first social experiment can be regarded as a consequence of, rather than a break with, its immediate past; rather like capitalism in relation to feudalism. Social change is a process of development and transformation which preserves certain features of the previous system in the new context. Many features of classical slavery persisted throughout feudalism and only vanished with the advent of capitalism. Similarly kinship societies did not necessarily create all the principles on which they were based; some were taken over from fraternities and gangs, and recombined with original elements. This, as we shall see, is what happened to exogamy and the prohibition of incest. Nonetheless the change was from animal to human society, or from a first non-specific human to a second specific human society. What is remarkable is that it was a double change: a social organization common to both primate and man became exclusively human. This is remarkable only for the repercussions it has had, not because it represents a total innovation.

The social process has changed and so has the natural. If we consider their joint evolution in human history, their discontinuity and independence vanish. Man incessantly revives their antagonism, moves their frontiers, reverses their respective values or establishes new relationships. But he can neither deny nature nor identify with society, for he belongs simultaneously to both. No part of humanity is or ever was more natural than any other. The desire to prove that man is a unique phenomenon is pointless, for the society and the nature he has created are only the latest in a series which, as far as we know, may go on for ever.

[VII]

Hunting and Kinship

1 *Social Repercussions of the Art of Hunting*

Primitive societies are based on kinship, that is to say on a network of relationships stemming from marriage and the family unit. Such societies are the natural outcome of evolving hunting skills which require specialized techniques and organized groups. Communality originally had as much bearing on consumption as on a rudimentary form of production. Monkeys and anthropoids feed independently; no sooner are they weaned than they have to be entirely self-reliant, and males, females, young and old generally have no mutual responsibilities. Their behaviour may be relatively concerted when searching for new feeding grounds or repulsing predators, but on all other occasions their actions are almost entirely independent. The advent of hunting and its separation from gathering utterly transformed living conditions. Though male and female activities were now distinct both groups had to provide for the whole community.

Moreover the human infant's slow maturation creates a link between the generations.[12] If we are to judge by Eskimo and Australian tribes, mothers would nurse their young for at least three years – partly, perhaps because of the increasing difficulty of providing sufficient food for ever larger communities. The men must instruct the youngsters in intricate physical and intellectual hunting skills. Thus parental responsibility is protracted, and in exchange ageing parents come to depend to some extent on their progeny when these are grown-up. As far as consumption is concerned groups, generations and sexes have become mutually dependent.

Hunting, unlike gathering and foraging, is a cooperative occupation, especially if the hunters are tracking down large game. Quite apart from its technical aspect (with which we are not concerned for the moment) it requires the cooperation and mutual reliance which already characterized all-male fraternities. The transition from gathering to hunting, like the transition from handicraft to manufacture, represents a socialization of means and ends, a concerted subordination of the parts to the whole. Hunting can be seen as an extension of reproduction so that apart from sexual reproduction it comes to include skills, implements and the environment, and at the same time as a communalization of this process of natural or human reproduction. The significance and the extension of social intervention to spheres which primate populations ignored, created a division of resources, activities and responsibilities on which relationships and organization were structured. Among Australian aboriginals clan membership is strictly regulated, and this is an organizational and not a territorial system of exclusions. Among the Bushmen and Eskimo memberships fluctuate according to the season and to the needs of each clan, as do the sites a clan appropriates for hunting or gathering. This mutual dependence is reflected in a number of other relationships and customs; for instance no one section of the community ever monopolizes goods permanently, excludes any individual from its undertakings permanently, or refuses to assist those who are in need or ill. Giving and receiving, and putting one's property at the disposal of others are the necessary conventions of a mutual partnership which makes comfort and survival possible.

Hunters cannot lead a sedentary life for long. In certain seasons of the year the males of different communities band together and set out in search of hunting grounds, which vary according to the game and to the time of year. Gathering expeditions also take place, though these are more restricted in scope since they include nursing mothers with their infants. But such nomadism is strictly motivated; as Clark observes:

> Since hunting-gathering communities depend entirely on the natural resources of their environment, their survival is in direct relation to the availability of adequate supplies. In consequence they cannot settle permanently in a given site but must be always on the move. During the rainy season they disperse to gather the berries and edible roots or plants which are then available; and during the dry season, when vegetation is scarce, they centre around permanent water-holes and probably resort to a purely carnivorous diet; thus the population follows its supplies. A lot has been said about pre-historic man's carnivorous habits, but vegetation certainly provided a means of satisfying his needs which was equally, and at first possibly more, important. A group of hunters would perhaps cover a territory measuring hundreds of square miles in the space of a single year, moving from place to place, eating berries and roots as these became available; for their meat supplies the population followed game, especially herbivorous herds, which leave the permanent water-holes during the rainy season and fall back on rivers and other permanent supplies when temporary supplies dry up. Such seasonal migrations are the rule for all hunting-gathering populations and correspond to the habits of the higher mammals as well. [13]

Nomadism is obviously determined by necessity and it has a positive social impact. Men and women exploit different aspects of their environment to make their respective contributions to the welfare of the family or clan; according to the season, each sex in turn becomes the main provider. The size of the community must of course correspond to these conditions. It cannot exceed a given density without exhausting local plant supplies, while hunting, to be fruitful, requires the cooperation of several families or clans. Thus periods of dispersal are followed by periods of reunion. Marcel Mauss has said that: 'Environment influences the population as a whole and not the individual,' [14] a fact which contemporary evidence substantiates.

Daryll Forde[15] provides some relevant examples from his observations of Blackfoot tribes who dwell on both sides of the Canadian border. They hunt the buffalo and follow its seasonal migrations. Towards the end of spring and the beginning of summer vast herds of these animals graze on the rich pastures of the north-west plains. With the coming of autumn the diminishing vegetation compels them to disperse into smaller, more mobile herds. The hunters adapt their tactics to the circumstances. In the summer they form large companies in order to tackle the herds grouped in the plains; in winter when supplies are limited they separate into small units spread over the territory, each providing for its own needs. These social units, constituted for a definite purpose, do not lose their identity when they join up into larger companies. Each has its own particular, naturally demarcated territory and its members are usually linked to the leader by some form of blood relationship. These seasonal fluctuations impart their rhythm to communal activity in general. Tribal assemblies take place in the summer when tents are erected, three or four deep, in a circular camp measuring some five hundred metres in radius. Each unit is allotted a more or less permanent site which it reclaims year after year. The successful outcome of the hunt is celebrated with rites and festivities while charms and amulets are bartered for skins and horses. The various male groups perform ritual dances and at a given time they all proceed to a specially built tent where, after much bargaining and discussion, clans exchange some of their members. The assembly then reaches its final climax in a ritual sun dance which sometimes goes on for a week. After this the community disbands and the clans take up their winter residence in the less fertile undulating western territory where they live in relative indepdendence.

The Netsilik Eskimo offer another example of alternating seclusion and sociability. They occupy the north and west of Hudson Bay. In June they disband into extended family groups to camp first on the shores, later further inland; they fish with harpoons and hunt caribou with bows and arrows. August sees the beginning of the salmon-fishing season. Large quantities of these fish are caught with tridents after the rivers have been blocked with dams. September is the time for caribou hunting in kayaks while in October salmon trout are caught through the thin ice that covers the rivers. Then the communities regroup for the seal hunt, when hunters are posted, harpoons poised, at every ice hole where, sooner or later, a seal will have to come up for breath. Winter is the season for social reunions, when groups of sixty or more members dwell in igloos on the frozen sea. Marcel Mauss has vividly described the cyclic rhythm of these communal relationships. During the long winter months the men, married or single, live in separate quarters from the women and children and spend their time indoors myth-making and story-telling. But in the summer family life reasserts itself. The compulsory and regularly recurring alternation between male communality and family autonomy creates a dual allegiance to both the public community and to a permanent private unit.

Animal and vegetable supplies do not only vary from season to season and from region to region. There are also years of plenty and years of famine when communal festivities and transactions must be deferred.[16] Yet, however protracted the periods of clan autonomy may be, the laws of hospitality serve to maintain the unity of the whole throughout these times of relative social independence. With the advent of nomadism the uninterrupted association of families and clans vanishes to be replaced by alternate periods of sociability and separation which preclude the establishment of inflexible hierarchies. On the other hand these families and clans are now dominated by dominated by a single complex, Society, on which they all depend for specific, seasonal supplies which can only be obtained through the cooperation of a considerable number of identically trained hunters and gatherers.

Furthermore the material division of hunting and gathering activities modifies the distinction between the sexes, on which it depends. From the purely biosocial sexual distinction common to primates, it becomes a difference in relation to the outside world. In primitive societies such as those of the sub-Arctic Ainu, male and female activities do not overlap to any significant extent. The women gather and collect in the vicinity of the settlement, while the male hunters range far afield. If the women do occasionally hunt they must be content to catch small animals that can be dispatched with sticks or even with their bare hands, since they are generally forbidden to handle their mates' weapons. They may sometimes be allowed to participate in the communal hunt, but only as beaters, and they are seldom, if ever, confronted with big game. In predominantly vegetarian populations where hunting is not a regular occupation, such as the Semang, sexual distinctions are not so obvious as they are in cynegenetic societies like the Kuchin. The latter, even when striking camp, separate into two groups: the heavily laden women lumber painfully along, heading straight for their destination; the men, carrying nothing but their weapons, explore the surrounding territory by roundabout ways.

For the African Lele the forest hunting grounds are an exclusively male reserve and the women cultivate groundnuts in the plains. Watanabe says: 'It seems to be certain that the differentiation of activity field according to sex is a universal phenomenon among modern food gatherers. It may be one of the ecological characteristics of man. Owing to differentiation the structure of man's home range differs from that of non-human primates.'[17]

This differentiation means the groups are complementary since neither can subsist without the other. More significantly it involves a separation which distinguishes most of our social institutions and customs to this day. Sexual inequality, which is the most remarkable consequence of differentiation, was determined by natural production. In order to obtain the balanced supplies required to satisfy communal needs, both male and female characteristics had to be develeped and both sexes had to be represented in sufficient quantity. The sexual aspect of what must already be seen as labour power emerged with all its significance.

The success of a hunting expedition depends on the number of hunters taking part as much as on their individual endurance and experience; a shortage of able hunters results in communal imbalance. Girls and boys must therefore be educated in quite different ways from early childhood and learn to conform to the behaviour of female and male adults respectively. They are made to inhabit two different worlds from the very start, each with its own tradition of experience and abilities.

Gathering remains a basically individual activity, but hunting tends to grow increasingly cooperative. As a result comradeship is more developed among males than among females. The seasonal reunions for hunting expeditions are male gatherings for a specifically male purpose, but they are the focus of social and material existence. Once the expedition is over the men return to the female world of gathering, occasional individual predacity and general autonomy. The rhythmic oscillation between a latent and an active formalized social life, the regular recurrence of lean and of plentiful months, reflects the basic differentiation where each term symbolizes one sex and stresses their inequality.

Apart from this ever-widening inequality, there has also been a reversal of primate and early hominid values. Formerly it was the young male who was the underprivileged, dispensable quantity; now the community's whole future depends on the adequacy and survival of young males. Luc de Heusch, discussing present-day kinship societies, describes what might well have been the situation in an early hunting community:

The young males have one definite advantage in cynegenetic societies: their labour power. This enables them to establish a dual relationship of reciprocity; first with the older males – they will obtain a bride from the matrilineal clan, probably the daughter of a maternal uncle; and second with their own age-group– from among these they will select a polyandrous companion or 'country bride'.[18]

For obvious reasons the adult human male no longer ignores his progeny, but on the contrary seeks to establish a firm relationship with them. With his sons this relationship must last long enough for him to transmit his dearly acquired knowledge and experience of game and wildlife in general. Unlike the gatherer and the beast of prey, he has every advantage in retaining these adolescents, whose defection to a rival clan would be a serious handicap. For the time, patience and energy spent in initiating the young hunter are not wasted; the clan as well as the youngster will profit from this initiation.

But now the girls are a dispensable quantity. According to a native informer: 'Parents often find they cannot afford to waste several years bringing up girls; we grow old so quickly that we must hurry up and have a son.' The young male's new status sets the parent-child relationship on an altogether firmer basis, particularly that between father and sons. This is an eminently human characteristic which has no parallel, in so far as we can tell, in simian communal organizations.

All these changes are interrelated and stem from a common root. The collectorization of the reproductive process, nomadism, and the division of activities and of resources reflect a single development which alters the significance of the environment and the organic potentialities of the species until the mode and structure of communal existence are radically transformed. There is no reason to believe that identical solutions were adopted everywhere. The diversity of prehistoric communities is partly due to a diversity in the social equipment of each. But kinship was undoubtedly a common development. The activities and conventions which these communities were the first to display correspond to, and can be explained by, its characteristics. We have seen that kinship, marriage and the prohibition of incest are pivotal features of these communities. Only the first is an innovation; the second reflects a new way of consolidating former relationships; and the third is the recasting of a law which was already operative in primate societies. None of these features depends on the others; they might each have occurred independently. But it is together that they constitute the basis for a specifically human pattern of domination and alliance.

2 *The Problem of Paternity*

(a) *The discovery of paternity*

These pivotal features first developed within the society of affiliation described in Chapter II. One of its main characteristics is the barrier between all-male non-reproductive sub-groups and heterosexual reproductive sub-groups. The former constitute a subordinate, distinct, indispensable category in a society dominated by a reproductive group whose male and female members may pursue different activities but maintain a regular heterosexual relationship. Within this group two units can be distinguished: the mother-child unit in which hierarchy is practically non-existent and which, notwithstanding the relatively brief duration of the strong mutual attachment it involves, rarely becomes a reproductive unit; and the reproductive unit consisting of one dominant male and one or more females. There is no positive link between young and adult males, and the former are treated as subordinates as soon as they reach a certain age.

From the evidence available to date it seems that primate societies of affiliation are characterized by male dominance, which is responsible for the permanent segregation of the non-reproductive males, and by the two units formed by a mother and her child and by a male and a female. As societies they are non-mediated, that is to say they are held together by a network of individual functions and tasks undertaken spontaneously without the intervention of any specialized social authorities. Their unity derives from individual necessity and not from an independent social structure. They have no resources other than those obtained by each member, and no rights over individuals, goods or territory. The community owns nothing in its own right and owes its existence to the lasting coordination and cohesion of its members.

Hunting gradually induced and required a certain amount of socialization. The two basic units of affiliation societies merged, and the whole group's reproductive and productive activities became indissolubly linked. Members of both sexes had to provide for the welfare of the community, and the different age groups became mutually dependent. J. H. Steward observes that: 'Although a nuclear family – a minimal unit of father, mother and children – is basic to all ethnographic cases, it may not have existed in early periods. The family among hunters and gatherers is based on strong sexual complementarity, men being primarily hunters and women carriers of wood and water, seed collectors, camp keepers and child tenders.' [19]

Thus the family became a necessary institution. It is generally supposed that the human infant's tardy maturation, making the father's presence indispensable to both mother and child, was responsible for its emergence. But such tardiness, or the dependence attached to it, is more than a simple biological phenomenon: it is a consequence of the natural and social evolution of the species. Protracted dependence would only increase the mother-child attachment were it not for the young male's necessary initiation which, naturally devolving to the father, would encourage paternal interest from the moment a boy was born. It seems irrefutable that the family unit was initially created around the male child.

The father's inclusion in the basic mother-child unit must have been one of the earliest problems which confronted society. It must certainly have been fraught with tensions, for among baboons and rhesus monkeys male aggressivity during the mating season often results in infanticide. Moreover the dominant male generally tends to separate a mother from her sons by banishing them to the periphery. Neither of these attitudes is conducive to the establishment of a permanent family relationship; that it was established nonetheless implies the creation of a father-son unit, equivalent to the basic mother-child unit, within the reproductive nucleus. This relationship would tend to be non-hierarchical, in contrast to the general trend of relationships between adult and young males, which probably still prevailed outside the family circle. Before the family as such emerged the young adolescent male's relationship to the female sub-group was one of equality and difference, while he was subordinate and undifferentiated in his relation to adult males. Paradoxical as it may seem, homosexual relations were the only sexual relations that had a social dimension; the submissive ritual of exposing the sexual organs is an example of this. If fathers and sons were to cohabit peacefully while the latter grew to maturity, such customs would evidently have to disappear. The problem was solved by instituting a hierarchy in the mother-child unit and creating an independent unit of adult and young males; in other words, a distance was introduced where none existed, and where it had previously prevailed it was now reduced. Paternity corresponds to an inclusion of masculine responsibility in a sphere where responsibility had been exclusively feminine. It involves boys in an alliance with their fathers and puts an end to the enforced banishment of young males from the inner circle. Kinship, which till then had been ignored, was now acknowledged.

A nuclear family generally consists of father, mother and children; but in some societies the father continues to be more or less an outsider, living apart in an all-male group and only joining his family at regular intervals. Rare instances of polyandry have also been noted where no real family exists. In the Trobriand islands polygamy is the rule rather than the exception, and the father is an intruder, or at least an accessory, in the mother-child unit. Among the Lele of Kasar he is often represented by a group rather than by a single male, a peculiarity which is reminiscent of affiliation societies, except that here the dominant males play the part of father-figures, individually or collectively. Affiliation turns into kinship when the father's natural relation to his children, and especially to his sons, is recognized as permanent, when he acquires a definite status in the family unit and when his lineage is added to or replaces the mother's. This is what distinguishes human from primate societies, or post-hunting from pre-hunting societies. Legally and ethically paternity is the general law. Marriage must precede conception or adoption if the children are to preserve their rights and avoid the fate of being branded as illegitimate or 'natural'; their social existence derives from their father. Conversely they give significance to their parents' union. In a number of societies an unfruitful marriage represents loss of status for its partners who will never join the ranks of the venerated ancestry. This explains the excessive importance accorded to individual fecundity in primitive societies even where infanticide is practised.

However when the family becomes an institution we find, instead of the problem of paternity, the problem of filiality: the problem of being the offspring of a mother and of a father, the one giving access to life, the other to society; of being related to the father through the mother and siding with him against her; or of seeing one parent as a rival and an intruder in the relationship formed with the other; in short the problem of experiencing a situation as unbearable, yet bearing it for the sake of security. In fact it is the institution of paternal ties that turns affiliation societies into societies of filiation.

(b) Celibacy, marriage and equality among men

'Again and again in the history of the world primitive tribes must have been clearly aware of the simple practical alternative; marry outside the clan or be exterminated.' Tylor's rather dramatic formula obviously represents a non-existent choice. Nonetheless it illustrates the fact that marriage is primarily a question of barter, and that the actual alliance is secondary. In the nomadic world the only way to ensure survival is to have access to the shelter of a foreign camp, that is to create mutually binding relations of hospitality outside the clan. The law of exogamy corresponds to such a necessity and is a natural consequence of the prohibition of incest. Both compulsory alliances and the prohibition of incest are acknowledgements of the family status and of marriage as a natural human condition.

In so-called primitive populations those who remain single are despised and underprivileged. They are often referred to by a derogatory or even insulting term and their status is generally no better than that of a cripple or a black magician, for they are guilty of sterility after having received the gift of life. 'What is more remarkable is the actual revulsion celibacy provokes in most societies. Generally speaking celibacy is non-existent in so-called primitive populations for the simple reason that an unmarried person cannot survive,' writes Claude Lévi-Strauss,[20] and he goes on to recall the case of an individual he met among the Bororos of Brazil, whose physical deterioration was obviously due to the deliberate neglect which is the fate of all celibates, rather than to the officially declared cause of disease.

In order to preserve them from such a fate families and clans make every effort to contract marriages between their sons and daughters as soon as possible. Preadolescent children of both sexes are formally engaged, and child-brides are given away to older men who undertake to maintain them until they reach nubility and can fulfil their matrimonial duties. This attitude to celibacy and to the advantages of heterosexual unions would almost suggest a certain natural reluctance towards marriage that had to be socially overcome. We tend to think of it as the logical outcome of the biological urges of each sex to be joined to its opposite, and we see the institution as a social means of controlling and sanctioning this urge, as a substitute for arbitrary mating, as the socialization of organic heterosexuality or as a human instead of an animal mode of reproduction. But such a view is biased and inaccurate in so far as the evolutionary stage of this substitution is concerned. For celibacy is compulsory in primate societies for all those who are excluded from sexual reproduction, while mating is highly hierarchized and far from promiscuous or disorganized. Most animal societies are based on distinctions between reproductive and non-reproductive individuals, and the opposition of bisexual to monosexual (normally male) sub-groups.

Observation of simian communities has revealed the significant role played by the all-male bands who are denied the right to establish permanent heterosexual relationships as a result of their inferior, segregated status. The single male is faced with a further problem: his ever-frustrated urge to participate in heterosexual groups in order to find a sexual partner and to enjoy all the advantages of dominance. Such a situation constitutes a threat to society, an endemic animosity between young, or subordinate, and privileged males. Thus the division characteristic of affiliation societies is two-edged. Moreover it is doubly incompatible with the specific conditions of a hunting community. In the first place the need for each hunter to rely on all the others implies that all males are more or less equal. In the second, the dominant males' constant obligation to protect their females from the advances of subordinates precludes lengthy expeditions; the unguarded females would certainly be abducted in their absence, for besides being sexual partners they are also symbols of the males' dominance. The introduction of hunting heralds a new relation between male age groups, and the abolition of segregation; every member of society must have free access to the reproductive group. Non-reproductivity continues to be a sign of temporary social inferiority, but it is no longer a status distinction permanently opposed to reproductivity. The matrimonial imperative reverses evolutionary tendencies and abolishes a form of discrimination which animal societies have preserved. Doubtless it commemorates the victory of the subordinate males, or the toppling of hominid social conventions.

Before it became a code of prohibitions and prescriptions dictating the choice of partners, marriage was a right and an obligation: the right of every individual to a sexual partner and descendants and the common obligation to make this possible. But rights tend to become obligations and obligations rights. Thus people must get married or the soundness of the rule will be invalidated. Society expects them to do their duty — and the only alternative is ostracism. In so-called primitive societies the right to sexual relations is similar to the right to vote; it puts an end to a state of inferiority and establishes equality in the place of inequality. Or semi-equality, to be more precise, since it concerns only the male contingent; the status of women remains unchanged. The bourgeois revolution's Liberty, Equality, Fraternity or Death only referred to the property owners; the Liberty, Equality, Fraternity or Death of the matrimonial revolution concerned only fathers, since in such societies being a man meant being a father. Thus marriage reflects a new aspect of paternity; it is the realization of a contract, an agreement between men for dealing with women and children. From this point of view it is a complete reversal of the principles on which affiliation societies were founded, for it enables the general public to enjoy what were formerly the privileges of an elite, that is of the reproductive couples.

3 *Sharing: Giving and Receiving*

'Give as much as you take and all will be well with you.' (Maori proverb).

(a) Conjugal exogamy

A man and a woman have to get married to start a family, and in most societies each must belong to a different family or clan. The obvious advantage of such a custom is that it establishes or consolidates alliances between different families and clans. But though its laws are unambiguous, the true significance of exogamy can only be surmised.

A society must exist before institutions or social categories can be created — unless, of course, these are seen as pre-established, natural systems of interpersonal or intercommunal relations, and not as part of the social structure that produced them. As we noted earlier, the family was established in an unmediated society which had no specific policy or economy and no framework of institutions to control its members. For such a society, the creation of large family units naturally allied to other families presents a considerable threat. Once the mother-child and reproductive units had merged, and the friction between males had been eliminated, the new unit thus constituted might, in theory, become wholly independent from the original society. And, since hunting depends entirely on a reliable, permanent association, such autonomy could have fatal consequences for the collectivity.

Moreover this novel and therefore subversive institution emerged, naturally enough, in a changing society where the community had ceased to be a compact whole in time and in space, enjoying direct and uninterrupted individual contact. 'Reunions' and 'dispersals' now depended on fluctuating ecological and productive factors, so that society as such was alternately a reality and an abstraction. Psychologically such conditions would encourage the revival of a common symbolic and historical heritage to maintain a unity that was periodically threatened by dispersal. Culturally it would promote the creation of customs and conventions to preserve and re-establish incessantly severed relations. On the other hand the society was obliged to enforce the dispersal of families and clans which, with their newly acquired requirements and habits, could no longer survive in a restricted territory where supplies would necessarily become inadequate. Interdependence therefore involved long priods of independence, while independence presupposed interdependence, that is the cooperation of every clan and family as soon as circumstances made such cooperation desirable.

These alternations, which correspond to the natural nomadism of such societies, represent, however, a potential danger. For during the periods of isolation clans could easily be cut off from the main body, or even join together independently to form a rival society. Relatively small clans would be particularly susceptible to such a risk. In a clan comprising about fifty members, or nine procreative couples, given the fertility rate of one child per couple every three years, there is little chance of more than three of these nine children surviving into adulthood; and the discrepancies between male and female survivors may be considerable. To reduce such discrepancies and enable the clan to procreate normally without resorting to polygyny, the best solution is to bring the total up to about five hundred members by merging with other clans. Otherwise demographic imbalance is inevitable.

A further source of demographic involution when the family constitutes the basic unit is the absence of marriageable partners or an excess of male children. In primate and hominid societies the problem is solved by banishing the non-reproductive members. But for the members of a society where marriage represents, apart from the acquisition of wife and children, a positive status symbol, and where intergeneration, and intersexual relations are strictly prescribed, the only solution is to merge with other clans. Incestuous unions are not an answer, since sons who marry their mothers or sisters do not escape from paternal control. In other words, if a relatively small clan becomes permanently isolated it can only revert to the promiscuity which is supposed to prevail in primate communities, but which, in fact, has no social significance for them; though it immediately acquires both reality and significance where the family is an acknowledged feature of the social structure. In human kinship societies its significance is obvious since they are productive as well as reproductive and if they are to survive they must include men and women in equal proportion and a sufficient general population to make the rotation from hunting to gathering practicable.

Thus an unmediated, nomadic society must simultaneously impose a limit to the larger multi-family clan's independence so that it does not escape social control altogether, and give it sufficient autonomy and freedom to enable it to fend for itself during regularly recurring periods. For their part such clans naturally strive to perpetuate their distinctive characteristics in an adequate social environment and will only submit to temporary isolation on the understanding that former relations will be regularly re-established. Such conditions are to the advantage of both parties since the society requires that all transactions taking place within or between clans should be concluded in its name and should favour its unity; while each clan requires that its isolation should be temporary, for it cannot afford to forego the right to be included in the communal structure which provides indispensable biological, material and intellectual contacts at regular intervals. Matrimonial alliances between different clans encourage this attitude, and by making them compulsory the society establishes itself as an indispensable entity. According to Lévi-Strauss exogamy provides the only means of maintaining the clan as such and avoiding the uncontrollable fragmentation and sub-division inbreeding would occasion; for customary or even over-frequent inbreeding would inevitably cause the society to 'explode' into a multitude of clans constituting as many closed systems or non-communicating monads whose proliferation and mutual antagonisms no pre-established unity could overcome.[21]

(b) Social endogamy and the impact of geneology

Society, as an intermittent yet stable structure, was periodically forced to disperse its elements in permanently constituted nomadic clans under conditions which, through sheer distance, threatened their mutual relations and thus the stability and unity of the society.[22] Exogamy, which requires that certain acts (such as intermarriage or eating specific foods) be forbidden within the clan, compels the various clans to share men, women, territories and supplies between them and thus to be mutually dependent. 'For a clan, a household, a group or a host is not free to abstain from demanding hospitality, accepting presents, trading or contracting matrimonial or blood alliances,'[23] writes Marcel Mauss.

The reciprocity thus established is reflected in the population's activities and welds together the different sections of the social structure so that surplus goods are consumed, needs are provided for, and all festivities and expeditions are communal. However the conditions attached to sharing are clearly prescribed. Clans are not free to contract alliances with whomsoever they choose: clan X marries its sons to the daughters of clan Y according to more or less strict regulations whereby the betrothed must conform to certain conditions of kinship, clan or status. More precisely, they must already be linked by previous alliances, for strangers do not contract marriages with strangers. Ancestry dictates the range of permissible unions which, depending on the society, can be modelled either on those of the parents or on those of the grandparents. A clan's exogamy is defined by the prohibition of unions within a given matrimonial category.

Preferential unions – or the prohibition to marry individuals outside a given category – determine the society's endogamy. There is no logical or historical motive for supposing that exogamy was preceded by a period of clan endogamy and inbreeding; such a custom would imply that the bride belonged to the clan as a whole, and there is no evidence of this in affiliation societies or in primitive communities. On the other hand a society's ascendancy over its factions represented by groups, clans or families is reflected in social endogamy, or the social restrictions which control matrimonial alliances. A family or group of families constitutes a unit within a wider system based on further obligations corresponding to status and locality. It is neither totally distinct and independent, nor is it one among a number of undifferentiated untis; each family is distinguished by its genealogy, and its alliances are more or less preordained. Genealogy and the inclusion within a motivated system involves synchronic and diachronic transactions which are distinct from other forms of trade and exchange: for each individual who is 'given away' another must be 'received', either simultaneously or at a later date, and alliances symbolize a general interdependence extending, through the generations, into the past and into the future.

But this hyper-organized system of alliances reflects the influence of a genealogy which transcends personal inclinations and everyday circumstances and subordinates private to general interests. The pattern of concluded marriages expresses the degree of each clan's allegiance to the whole structure. The boundaries of continually revived genealogical relationships are the boundaries of socity itself, since beyond these mutual links alliance, language and communality do not exist. The regular distribution of human beings which ensues reveals the influence of a very concrete entity: the genealogy of each successive generation. Under its influence marriage is not simply the union of one man to one woman, nor even of one clan to another. It is a union mediated and concluded by parents who, besides dictating the relationship, provide the goods. It represents the alliance of one generation against the next, and a strict social control which combines reciprocal exchanges with hierarchical divisions and turns kinship into alliance and alliance into kinship. Its field of action is the family where personal relationships concluded within prescribed conditions provide the basis for the exercise of authority and law. Thus the family evolved and was incorporated into society, while society took the family as model and became a society of kinship.

(c) The generalization of exogamic sharing

Exogamy was responsible for this modification. Its influence was not restricted to matrimonial conventions; it reflected a general tendency to share which is peculiar to primitive societies. The same tendency is expressed in the custom of blood-brotherhood, for instance, whereby men of the same age group but different clans agree to a permanent relationship of mutual assistance and reliance similar to that of real brothers, and seal the agreement with each others' blood.[24] The obvious advantage of such a relationship is that, when travelling abroad, each partner can expect the same reception from his 'brother's' clan as he would receive from his own; it has to be sanctioned by each participant's clan before it can be concluded. The alliance is then contracted like a wedding, and accompanied by ceremonial rites and an exchange of gifts. Each of the 'brothers' undertakes to avoid committing adultery with the other's wife and to prefer him to any other prospective suitor for his daughter's hand. When one visits the other he expects to receive food, weapons and any gift he may choose to demand, as well as protection against eventual aggressors and a share in all hunting spoils.

Certain aspects of initiation rituals reflect the same tendency. In Australia a youth's initiation must be attended by his direct male relatives, but also by his maternal uncle, his father's second cousin, who is usually also his brother-in-law, and a member of his future wife's clan, each of whom represents a different territorial clan from his own. Initiation takes at least two years during which time the young man is under the guidance of an adult male, for example his brother-in-law, who instructs him in the art of hunting and other exclusively male skills, in exchange for the product of his pupil's hunting or gathering activities. The initiator's relationship with his pupil is similar in many ways to his relationship with his wife (who may be the boy's sister). Indeed both pupil and bride have frequently been mistaken for child-slaves by missionaries, and young girls and boys were commonly kidnapped in Groote Englandt, the former to serve as brides, the latter as unpaid labourers.

Circumcision rituals have a similar setting and require the same participants. In Australian Nambuti tribes the boy's future father-in-law performs the operation assisted by a couple of his maternal uncles. The ceremony is called *ulkuteta,* meaning adoption, and links the boy permanently to his circumciser; the pair now communicate by means of an esoteric idiom and have sexual relations until the boy attains manhood and marries the older man's daughter. In other tribes the future father-in-law keeps the foreskin which he ultimately returns to his son-in-law on the latter's wedding day.[25]

The conventions attached to such alliances as well as those related to the sharing of certain hunting grounds or resources conform to a system of identical rules. Durkheim was perfectly justified when he said that he believed they all bore the mark of an exogamy which predated and included all other primitive social institutions. He assumed however that these societies had at a given time possessed a complee set of integral and more or less stable institutions. It is on such an assumption that reconstructions are attempted of a synchronic system of social, ethical and ritualistic conventions whose peculiar dynamics were eradicated by colonialism. In primitive societies the sharing of individuals, property, time and energy between clans derives from a principle which is perculiar to exogamy, much as the principle of profit and productivity infiltrates the whole social body of capitalist society. A portion of the produce, energy, territory and offspring of each clan or individual is reserved for the community, so that social ties are constantly renewed while giver and taker participate equally in what is given and in what is received. Marcel Mauss observes: 'The communion and alliance thus created are relatively indestructable. In fact, this symbol of communal life – or the enduring significance of shared goods – only reflects more or less directly the way in which the sub-groups of segmented, primitive forms of society permanently overlap and are mutually indebted to each other for all they possess.'[26]

The practice of giving and the expectancy of reciprocity are two facets of a single principle: giving to receive. Since it is in the interest of the community that everyone should be provided for, each individual is required to supply his neighbour, and the possessions to which each member is entitled must be shared to ensure equality. In this respect sharing is a substitute for the purely coordinative form of distribution proper to affiliation societies where the community only intervenes to establish a limit within which every member gets what he needs or desires. Once accumulation and property reach the point where production and reproduction are independent, men cease to be shared as possessions and are instead exchanged for these; sharing becomes exchange, or the transfer of possessions for people at an established rate. In sharing, what is offered and what is received represent a desired dependence; it is a synthetic operation in which each transaction is more than the simple transfer of specific goods – of a gift and its equivalent. In exchange the process is reversed and the two participants retain their independence by paying back what they have received so that neither owes the other anything. It is an analytic operation in which each transaction is the transfer of equivalent, though different goods, of a possession and its symbol. Sharing introduces continuity into disconnected actions, compels the participants to deal with each other, pursues an equitable, long-term restitution and establishes a right to future goods. Exchange breaks continuity, frees the participants from ulterior obligations, accepts short-term restitution and restricts all rights to immediate goods only. In the first case necessities are given; in the second superfluities are conceded. In the first goods mediate unions; in the second they are objects of discord. But perhaps men had to learn dependence and bondage before they could appreciate independence and freedom, and had to practise alliance and reciprocity before they could enter into transactions by contract.

The institution of family and exogamy, or the principle of sharing which preceded exchange, obviously helped to undermine the structure of those primate-type societies of affiliation which were already in the process of being transformed by communalization and nomadism. The impact of immediacy diminished with the alternate dispersal and reunion of the community. In the midst of isolation and independence symbolism tends to permeate reality, enabling the society to preserve the significance of union and dependence. On the other hand once the clans are united and dependent again reality takes on symbolic overtones. Hence the emotion connected with reunions and departures, the exaggerated rituals and celebrations in primitive societies; it is as if everyone had to get rid of a load of unspoken words and repressed gestures, and simultaneously store up words and gestures for the long months of silence and solitude. Memory is the guardian and the essence of social existence and vice versa, so that actions signify the past in the present, others in the self and the community in the individual. Society thus evolved from a history that was simply lived to a history that was experienced, before it emerged into a history that it made. During this intermediary stage it set out on a new track where physical independence was necessary but where society became an idea, a powerful symbol of unity. Yet the distances between generations and sexes which had preceded the emergence of man were preserved and became that elaborate system of kinship which formed the basis of human relationships.

[VIII]

Women in a Male Society: The Problem of Incest

1 *Why Women?*

There is no obvious reason why the exogamic pairing of the members of a society, known as marriage, should result in the inequality of the sexes, but the fact is that it is the men who share out the women amongst themselves. The prohibition of incest is an expression of such discrimination. Incest is condemned in most societies and not many people would commit it willingly. Its prohibition has served as a model for all the prohibitions society has ever decreed. The interest it has aroused is wholly justified for it is a phenomenon which has profoundly influenced human society and the human psyche.

Claude Lévi-Strauss in his *Elementary Structures of Kinship* starts from the premise that whenever a basic product is in short supply society must ration its consumption to ensure its fair distribution; since man has always had to contend, not only with inadequate food supplies, but also with a shortage of women, the prohibition of incest corresponds to such a rationing:

> It decrees that the social value of women is not dependent on their natural distribution. Therefore what it does depend on has to be defined. To borrow a current modern (but really ageless) commercial term applied to 'rare commodities' in general, the practical purpose of the prohibition is to 'freeze' women within the family circle so that they can be distributed or contended for by the community and under its control, rather than under that of a closed system. This aspect is the only one which has been studied so far: but it is obviously the main aspect, and the only one which is coextensive with the prohibition as a whole.[27]

The custom of giving a daughter or a sister to another man so that he will be obliged to give his daughter or his sister in return becomes meaningful and necessary when it is considered as the 'freezing' of a scarce commodity, the sacrifice of immediate for future satisfactions, of personal to communal interests. 'Thus all the negative stipulations of the prohibition are counterbalanced by positive ones. The prohibition is equivalent to an understanding that sacrifices will be made good.' [28] Marriage as a means of sharing goodwill and possessions, including women, warrants the sacrifice.

Through this compulsory sharing strangers become relatives and potential enemies become comrades. The transfer of women is more than the simple shunting of dispersed persons; it provides a means of establishing social connections. Generally acknowledged exogamic laws constitute the code of rules set up by the society as a whole and respected by all. The custom of giving and receiving brides and gifts is dictated by mutual self-interest but it has a generous aspect too, and the pre-established rituals and pomp with which it is surrounded make it a memorable, exciting public occasion. However the transaction on which it depends is based on symbolic thought. It had to be preceded by language and reflects a departure from nature. As Lévi-Strauss writes:

> The emergence of symbolic thought required that women, like words, should be exchanged. Indeed, in this case, it was the only way to overcome the ambiguity involved in seeing the same woman as two incompatible beings: one, the object of personal sexual and possessive desires; the other, the potential object of another man's desires, and thus a means of obtaining beneficial alliances and connections. [29]

Both aspects of the prohibition are reflections of the masculine mind. By including women among their possessions and supplies it withholds and forbids; by enabling them to barter and to contract social connections that will help to ensure the survival of the clan it liberates and concedes. It stipulates unambiguously both who represents the clan in the mutual agreement and who dictates the formalities of such an agreement. Obviously these are men. The shortage of women which gives them a high rarity value and turns them into prized possessions simultaneously excludes them from the sphere of all-important communal relationships. Their status in the Trobriand Islands as described by Malinowsky is far from exceptional: 'Since the women are excluded from the exercise of power, can neither own land nor enjoy a number of other privileges, they cannot take part in tribal meetings or public debates concerning agriculture, hunting, fishing, sailing, ceremonial rituals, celebrations or dances.' [30] Women are male status symbols. They advertise a man's virility, and their own social existence is consequently diminished. Yet, according to Lévi-Strauss, a woman cannot be a symbol and nothing but a symbol, for in a masculine world she is nonetheless a person and in so far as she is a symbol she must be acknowledged as a maker of symbols. In the masculine matrimonial discourse a woman is never simply that which is discussed; for if women in general represent a given type of communication, each woman preserves the singular value arising from her ability to play her part in a dialogue before and after marriage.[31]

Through such a dialogue – made possible by the regulations of an alliance over which they have no sway – women are ultimately the transmitters of natural signs. They belong to nature, and are therefore, as a rule, situated on the margins of culture or outside it. Eve's dialogue with the serpent inspired the revealing rabbinic comment that Woman had knowledge and understanding of animal speech, a knowledge and an understanding which was apparently denied to Man. The distinction is an accepted fact which is reflected in the bonds of kinship: The complex business relationship constituting marriage is not established between a man and a woman each of whom gives and receives something but between two male groups for whom the woman represents an object of the transaction and not one of the partners in this transaction. This is true even though the girl's feelings are generally respected. Such an attitude can be found in all societies, including our own where marriage figures as a personal contract.[32]

Reciprocity is the general basis for all individual and collective transactions and relationships, but it is an exclusively male prerogative and it concerns only the male members of society; women have no part in it. Lévi-Strauss observes that sexual relationships in the Trobriand Islands are seen as a service women do to men. The lack of reciprocity which characterises them here, as in most human societies, is a consequence of a general phenomenon: the reciprocity on which marriage is based was not established between men and women but between men by means of women, who are only its main motive.[33] And he suggests that this is because: in human societies women enjoy neither the same status nor the same rank as men. We cannot ignore this fact without failing to perceive that it is men who exchange women, and not vice-versa.[34]

I have quoted these observations at some length because they appear to throw light on the prohibition of incest from what seems to me is the most significant angle. It is obvious that the prohibition affects two different levels. On the one hand it compensates, theoretically, for the uneven distribution of that supposedly rare commodity, women. On the other it sanctions and expresses the social disparity of the sexes, turning a quantitative discrepancy of numbers into a qualitative discrepancy of status. A woman who abstains from sexual intercourse with her next of kin, unlike a man, is entitled to no compensatory privilege such as receiving another man in exchange for the one she has given up. On the other hand a man acquires a bride from another man, not from a woman, and women never associate freely with men as equals. The world of men and the world of women circle in different orbits and in opposite directions. Men inhabit a universe of signs and women a universe of significance. Men achieve marriage through alliance and for them kinship is a means: women achieve alliance through marriage and kinship is their purpose. If the prohibition of incest marks the transition from nature to culture it is a transition from a state of male and female equality to a state of male dominance. The prohibition, like all forms of social intervention, creates a dual set of relationships: reciprocity for the men and subordination for the women, the second being one of the conditions for the first.

2 *Natural Law or Social Rule?*

Though it is clear that the prohibition of incest establishes an unequal relationship between two elements of a society, this aspect is generally overlooked, and the prohibition is seen as a physical law created by man on behalf of nature and applied uniformly to a series of objective processes or elements — such as women, men, instincts, sexual behaviour or genetic phenomena. James Frazer wrote:

> The law only forbids men to do what their instincts incline them to do. What nature itself prohibits and punishes, it would be superfluous for the law to prohibit and punish. Accordingly we may always safely assume that crimes forbidden by the law are crimes which many men have a natural propensity to commit. If there was no such propensity there would be no such crimes, and if no such crimes were committed what need to forbid them? Instead of assuming, therefore, from the legal prohibition of incest that there is a natural aversion to incest, we ought rather to assume that there is a natural instinct in favour of it, and that if the law represses it, as it represses other natural instincts, it does so because civilised men have come to the conclusion that the satisfaction of these natural instincts is detrimental to the general interests of society.[35]

This law concerns relationships between given individuals who owe nothing to it while it adds little to them. Such relationships develop according to a certain pattern because they unite diverse elements, that is opposite sexes each with its specific intellectual and physical characteristics. The reciprocity or non-reciprocity and the social inclusion or exclusion resulting from this law depend on the intrinsic value of these elements. And since the law dictates the relationship between two distinct beings and simply combines heterogeneous elements, it duplicates circumstances it has not created, or objective phenomena which, through its purely intellectual and practical intervention, cease to be arbitrary, while it confers universality and independence on those who decree and impose it. The prohibition of incest has acquired the inevitability of the law of gravity or of natural selection. It is assumed that because of the action of this law there can be normal, regular relations established between the sexes and natural incestuous desires are abolished. But it is not difficult to refute these assumptions.

To begin with it is impossible to speak of incest where kinship is not recognized as such. We have no reason to suppose that the prohibition operated among hominids and is therefore coextensive with the human race, inseparable from its social organization. Was it created in response to a shortage of women? Such an explanation becomes plausible if we identify society anthropologically with kinship in the same way as we identify it economically with trade. The common factor is exchange which, in both cases, presupposes a limited supply of interchangeable goods. However whereas in the economy such goods are of various kinds, in the family only women answer the specification. The one purpose of a transaction of this sort is to achieve a balance involving the agents, or independent owners, in a relationship of reciprocity. The attitude of mind which dictated matrimonial laws, conceiving woman as a means of communication in a masculine society, is very similar to that which incites buyers and vendors to value merchandise with a view to collective rather than personal profit. The prohibition of incest in matrimonial exchanges, like the rules of ownership in trade, decrees who is entitled to give and to receive, to bid and to offer; it dictates the rules of the game and selects the players.

Rarity value is theoretical rather than actual; it results from the actions of those who require it for specific purposes. As Robert Jaulin says, the laws of kinship 'are only significant within a cultural whole, in the framework of a given mode of existence'.[36] In most societies girls and boys are born in equal numbers and their eventual disparity is due to various factors such as infanticide, polygyny or the monopoly of girls by the elders of the tribe. If primate societies are anything to go by we may assume that females would originally have been quite as numerous as males and that they were equally shared out.

In other words the rarity of women in primitive societies was very probably contrived deliberately as a result of matrimonial laws, just as traders create shortages to raise or to maintain the value of certain goods. The men, acting according to the rules of commerce, did not share their womenfolk because they were rare, but created the rarity for the purpose of sharing them to better advantage. The result would be the same if the definition of exchange were reversed and if it were assumed that a society generally tries to get rid of what it produces in excess; the value of women would decrease in proportion to their availability and they would be exchanged for more valuable goods. There exists, to our knowledge, at least one example of such behaviour in tribes where the elders monopolize the women and concede them to the younger men in exchange for pre-established advantages.[37]

Thus the prohibition of incest cannot be explained conclusively by fluctuations in demographic numbers. These might well have been a consequence of the prohibition as the coveted goods were alternately stored and freed. The explanation would then have to be sought elsewhere than in the presocial circumstances which were responsible for such conditions. Paradoxically enough, if this had been the case, incest would have been a necessary and accepted means of tiding over until the time when women could be profitably put on the market again, just as polyandrous relations are a temporary solution until young men have reached a marriageable age.

Can it then be asserted that the purpose of the prohibition is to avoid inbreeding[38] and thus preserve a vigorous population? The answer is no. The prohibition only applies to officially acknowledged, not actual consanguinity and is not a valid means of protection against the eugenic danger of endogamic unions. Unions sanctioned by the law vary from one society to another, and are mainly a question of convention. In some populations the marriage of a foster brother and sister is forbidden. In others a great-uncle can marry his great-niece. Among the Iatmul[39] marriages with classificatory 'sisters' are common, and if the clan becomes too endogamic a law is made, decreeing that half the population belongs to the prow of the war pirogue and the other half to the stern; thus the problem is solved.

There is evidence that incest is not universally condemned. Even where it is prohibited by law and custom it is in fact far more widely practised than we tend to admit.[40] It would seem that the laws of exogamy and the prohibition of incest are relatively independent one of the other.[41] As to the theory that sexual partnerships are permitted or forbidden in order to protect society against a state of 'natural' promiscuity, we now know that it is groundless.

There is a general tendency to see the prohibition of incest either as a means of improving or maintaining the species, or as a means of repressing primitive instincts. In fact the permanent union of individuals is always subjected to rules and regulations, but these vary enormously from one society to the next. Conventions are usually dictated by necessity or convenience, and psychology and biology must make the best of them. Incest is the product of such conventions. Its roots are buried in the society that forbids it, and the object of such a prohibition is neither biological nor psychological.

3 *The Only Real Incest: That of the Mother*

The prohibition's significance is not related to psychological, biological or demographic imperatives, nor is it a means of avoiding conflicts within a restricted group. Most other species appear to coexist peacefully without it. On the other hand we know that most human societies discriminate between incestuous and non-incestuous relations and that incest occupies a place on their scale of values. From this we can assume that the prohibition is general, and its absence or transgression become all the more significant: far from invalidating the general rule they confirm it.

Such exceptions, of which compulsory incest for certain classes of a society is the most notable, are not arbitrary inversions of a general rule or a sign of wilfulness and perversity. Compulsory incest, as a specific means of defining the relations between social groups, is as valid as the prohibition, if less common. The significance of such a compulsion and its acceptance by the community does not correspond to an arbitrary distortion of the prohibition any more than writing that starts at the right-hand side of the page or boustrophedon writing has any connection with the mirror-writing of a dyslexic person or the secret cypher used by Leonardo da Vinci. In the highly civilized societies where it occurs it is mainly a prerogative of the ruling classes. In Cambodia the aristocracy are allowed to contract incestuous marriages. In Persia marriages between father and daughter or brother and sister were frequent, but the surviving documents do not reveal whether the custom was restricted to the upper classes or not. In Madagascar most incestuous unions are forbidden to the lower classes, but among the nobility only sexual intercourse with the mother is prohibited. In Peru the Incas married their sisters. In Polynesia if the firstborn is a girl she is married off to the youngest son to avoid conflicts over leadership. Incestuous unions were common in Ancient Egypt, and not only among the Pharaohs. In Samoa a nobleman can marry his sister but not his mother or his daughter. In Hawaii a chieftain's rank was calculated according to the incestuous unions of his forebears and those which he himself contracted; the union considered most worthy and sacred was that of a high-ranking full brother and sister, and their offspring were worshipped as gods. In a wider context all James Frazer's 'divine' kings have one thing in common: they are the issue of incestuous parents and commit ritual incest particularly with their mothers; such, indeed, is the condition of their kingship.

Luc de Heusch has carefully analysed the real and symbolic aspects of this widespread, institutionalized compulsion.[42] Though experienced as a violation of the norm and acknowledged as such, it is precisely as a violation that it acquires the significance of an exemption from social restrictions, and involves further violations like eating forbidden foods or even committing murder. Infringing rules and committing crimes against that which otherwise constitutes the framework of communal solidarity invests those who do so with a magical aura and sets them above the populace. But this only applies to the chosen few. If ordinary mortals commit such transgressions they are rejected by society as sub-human beasts. Thus the aristocrat defines his rank, asserts his priorities and refuses to associate with the lower classes as exogamy frequently requires.

In this way a forbidden act — marriage with a blood relation — divides society in two: on one side the sacred, if somewhat unproductive elite, and on the other the profane, inferior masses. Compulsory incest establishes, effectively or symbolically, a relative equality of the sexes in the ruling classes where the laws of kinship are overruled by a quasi sacred order. They are free to adopt the customs of the masses if they choose, but the reverse is impossible. The people are made to realize their inferiority, and understand that they should be prepared to give daughters, goods or services without receiving anything in exchange. Compulsory incest can therefore not be seen as a negation of the prohibition, for it turns the prohibition into a means of classifying human categories.

The prohibition itself is enforced with different degrees of strictness, and it is always more relentless for women than for men. According to Malinowski, for the communities of the Trobriand islands:

> Incest with one's mother is considered a truly horrible crime, but the taboo weighs quite differently on a brother and sister. . . . It must be remembered that, though incest between father and daughter is frowned upon, it is not referred to by the pejorative term *surasova* (clan exogamy or incest as such) and is not supposed to provoke ill-health. [43]

A scale of the social values common to most populations could be obtained by recording the various forms the prohibition assumes, the opprobrium different aspects of incest arouse, and the sanctions which transgressions of the prohibition entail. The form of incest most generally condemned is undoubtedly that between mother and son; between fathers and daughters it is most easily tolerated. Freud believed that there was every reason to assume that the prohibitions of the totem were directed against the son's incestuous desires. [44] And he noted that the first restrictions which the introduction of matrimonial categories involved concerned the sexual freedom of young men (that is incest between brother and sister or son and mother) and that it was only extended later to include a father's incestuous relations with his daughter.' [45]

Though the exemption is not official, in most cases an incestuous father is seen as merely reprehensible whereas a mother is condemned outright. We are only too familiar with such discrepancies in the enforcement of laws; they show that a society is made up of those who dictate the law and those who suffer it and against whom it is directed. Prohibitions invariably reflect the social inequalities they enhance, and the prohibition of incest is no exception. It clearly divides those who must never under any circumstances commit incest from those who may, or in certain cases, must commit it. Thus class distinctions are created.

In the various societies we have discussed the prohibition aims at discriminating between the aristocrats, or leaders, and the common people, fixing their respective privileges and obligations and deciding who are the givers and who the receivers. In primitive societies it serves the same function on a reduced scale. Its significance – already latent in kinship societies – first emerged in the earliest political, state-controlled structures. But this occurred precisely because it had the potential aptitude to create a difference, to define categories and maintain distinctions: on the one hand the commodities (women, the masses, adolescents); and on the other the consumers (men, the elite, adults).

If the prohibition of incest is seen as the repression of sexual instincts, a means of regulating sexual choice, it must be admitted that this only applies to the instincts and choice of women, for they and not incest represent a threat. Similarly the repression of violence and aggression in civilized societies is directed against particular sections of these societies such as adolescents or the underprivileged. Violence and aggression are admissible, or anyway tolerated, elsewhere. In other words, once a law has been accepted by society – whether it is inscribed on tables or in the memory of man – it becomes a means of distinguishing between social categories by defining the roles and characteristics of each.

4 *Laws of Kinship, Laws of Dominance*

The prohibition of incest is thus discriminative and hierarchic. According to the laws of kinship women are exchanged on the one hand as goods and obligations and on the other as symbols of such goods and obligations. But raw materials, human or otherwise, cannot become objects or symbols of exchange without the intervention of a whole system of rules and regulations. The art of turning one section of society into a commodity, while another section sets itself up as the producer of such a commodity is a common occurrence. Slavery is one example of the art of acquiring ascendancy. It is a status symbol for the owners and a sign of deprivation for the owned, and has no civic reality other than that of classifying 'human herds' as the property of others. Aristotle says:

> So any piece of property can be regarded as a tool, enabling a man to live; and his property is an assemblage of such tools including his slaves. . . . Tools in the ordinary sense are productive tools, whereas property is useful in itself. . . . Now life is action not production, therefore the slave as property is one of these [tools] that minister to action. . . . A piece of property is sometimes spoken of as a part; for a part is not only part of something but wholly belongs to it: . . . any

human being that by nature belongs not to himself but to another is by nature a slave.[46]

The proletarian is better off in that he at least has freedom of choice, but in every other respect he is a marketable commodity. Lacking capital he has only his labour power which he sells to the highest bidder, and he is at the mercy of price fluctuations and redundancy, with emigration as the only alternative.

Capitalist social relations and the law of profit continually produce this commodity which, with the help of the political, ideological and social apparatus, is always ruled by the owners of wealth.

In most societies arbitrary classifications of this kind are to be found even among the liberal professions. And in primitive societies where men and women have distinct occupations – hunting for the men and gathering for the women – the customary, institutionalized and mythologized inequality of the sexes might possibly correspond to the need to maintain each section in its appropriate function. Though this is not the place to pursue such analogies, it is impossible to ignore the similarity between the status of these primitive women and that of the proletariat, slaves and so on who represent goods or symbolize exchange values. As Lévi-Strauss observes: The third volume of this series will complete the demonstration of the fact that this is an absolutely basic feature of the myths we are now considering, and that those myths shed light on a decisive stage in human thought, which is attested in innumerable other myths and rites the world over. It is as if, in bringing about the mystic submission of women to their authority, men had, for the first time but in a still symbolical way, grasped the principle which would one day allow them to solve the problems created by the numerical dimensions of society; as if, in subordinating one sex to the other, they had evolved a blue-print of the genuine, but as yet inconceivable or impracticable solutions, such as slavery, which would involve the subjection of certain men to the domination of other men.[47]

Whatever the context in which woman was first subdued, the similarity of the circumstances throughout history and the specificity of the distinctions – of class or of productive power – preclude the possibility of such a condition being natural; it is society which has selected her for this part. If women represent gifts or an exchange value in matrimonial relations just as labour power represents a commodity in commodity transactions, this is because the social system to which each belongs requires that they should be such. The mind of man can shape and refine social structures, fitting each category into its appropriate pigeon-hole, but it cannot influence the orientation of these categories which is obviously not organically predetermined. The prohibition of incest in a kinship society stresses social division and transforms the laws of kinship into coordinates of a 'motivated distinction' between men and women.

Reciprocity here is based on its opposite, and masculine equality depends on female submission. Dominance is certainly not foreign to primitive societies, for as Nietzsche said: 'He who seeks a beginning will always find more remote beginnings.'

[IX]

The Sex Struggle

1 Two Societies in One

(a) The society of secrecy

Broadly speaking primitive societies are structured around two main axes: distinctions between kin and non-kin, and the sexual dichotomy of male and female which pervades all social activities from living conditions to language. Both distinctions are involved when an individual, confronted with the choice between what is licit and what is not, has to differentiate between his family and others and between himself and another. The conventions of kinship define the groups of individuals who can intermarry or not according to the social conventions. In certain societies a man's children can marry his sister's children but not his brother's, while marriage between the offspring of two sisters is forbidden. This rule is not general, nor is it always so explicit, but it is common enough to prove that kinship and social sexual hierarchy are related. Such a hierarchy does more than simply juxtapose two categories according to sex; in some respects it is a matter simply of separation but in others it is a matter of discrimination to man's advantage. Men establish relationships which give them the means, status and authority to tip the scales their way and keep them there. Masculine dominance and solidarity are basic features of primitive ideology, economy and policy. The existence of more or less secret male societies, and the absence or inefficiency of a female equivalent, is a relatively common phenomenon. It has been observed in Melanesia, Black Africa, North America, Malaysia, Polynesia and elsewhere.

In a Blackfoot tribe there may be as many as a dozen such societies. They are known generically as 'all comrades' but each has a particular name of its own, and caters for members of a specific age group who are promoted every four years or so. Though these promotions occur simultaneously during the summer general reunion, they constitute individual transactions involving horses, weapons and clothes and entitle the candidate to the rank and the insignia of his predecessor who has had to bargain for a corresponding promotion. At four-yearly intervals all but the elders accede to a higher rank, while the youngsters are enrolled for the first time in the lowest-ranking society. These societies are responsible for the planning of summer expeditions and encampments. The head-men submit the plans they have drawn up to the tribal chiefs who make the final choice. Members of two or three societies whose projects have been selected are put in charge of the expedition and pitch their tents in the middle of the camp which they take turns in patrolling by night. They also have to keep track of herd migrations and organize the hunt which is the real purpose of the expedition. The frequent rotation of responsible positions occupied by these men, on whom the tribal chiefs rely implicitly in cases of emergency, precludes the risk of their assuming dominant roles in the community and thus threatening established power.

These secret societies appear to exert a considerable influence, and since they are centres for public cults and initiation rites they tend to acquire a religious aura.[48] The links which unite the members of such societies are frequently stronger than those between clan members.[49] In Australia men from different clans assemble for secret ceremonies from which women and all non-initiates are strictly excluded; as a result the men of the Castor clan, for instance, will be closer to those of the Eagle-Vulture, Bat, Crow or Frog clans with whom they constantly associate, than to those members of their own clan who are excluded from their particular society.

(b) Sexual discrimination

The segregation of the sexes is further reflected in eating habits. For instance while neither men nor women are allowed to consume the flesh of a clan totem animal, among the Yualarois no woman, whatever her clan, is allowed to eat the brown vulture. Among the Banks Islanders sexual discrimination is probably more prominent than anywhere else. Here the men eat and sleep at the *sukwe* (or club). If one of them is excluded he is forced to eat with the women and thus become an object of general contempt. To put an end to his 'ignominy'[50] he must bribe a friend to help him to be readmitted. Such societies usually possess sacred objects or masks which the general public can only glimpse at public meetings or processions from which the women are totally excluded. Referring to the Iatmul of New Guinea, Bateson writes that: 'When women take part in a ceremony they are conscious of doing something which, though normal for men, is quite exceptional for them. thus on these exceptional occasions they adopt elements of masculine culture behaving like men and wearing the ornaments generally reserved for them.'[51]

The presence of these exclusive secret societies confirms the fact that in primitive communities power is always in the hands of the men. They do not only assemble for hunting and ritual purposes; their functions include enforcing the communal laws they have decreed which obviously aim at isolating and subduing the women. Not only do men and women usually eat apart, consuming different foods, but among the Guyacurus and in the Caribbean Islands each sex uses a different vocabulary. In a number of tribes, such as those of the Mortlock Islands, the clansmen sleep in a communal house in the centre of the village surrounded by smaller huts for the women and girls who, belonging to a different clan, are not allowed to share the men's quarters. In California the Hupa women occupy the family dwelling but the men only join them for meals, retiring at nightfall to the Turkish baths where they spend the night; however, segregation is often relaxed during the summer. Regulations of this sort are most strictly observed by the Marquesas, Solomon and Banks Islanders. In Alaska Eskimo women are excluded from the men's communal dwellings and the Northern Athapaskan even segregate boys and girls. This attitude permeates every detail of tribal activity where, as Geza Roheim says: 'The men are united in the cult of an object which is the representation of a penis, and the women are banished from their presence.'[52] Samoy males are forbidden to touch objects that have been used by women. Bushmen believe that they will lose their virility if they sit on the side of the camp reserved for the women. The avoidance of any contact with menstrual blood is of course a common phenomenon. The laws dividing the sexes are enforced from an early age and become stricter at adolescence when, in many cases, brothers and sisters are not allowed to speak to each other. Among the Lethas of Burma girls and boys must even avoid looking at each other if they happen to meet.

Emile Durkheim asserted that the link between such prohibitions and exogamy is obvious. The latter consists in a similar prohibition of contact: it forbids sexual intercourse between men and women of the same clan. The sexes must be kept as strictly apart as the sacred and the profane, and the slightest infringement of such a rule provokes as much horror as the violation of a taboo. As with established taboos, such infringements are either formally penalized by the community or the punishment is automatically incurred by the culprit as a natural result of the powers involved — a fact which implies that exogamy is based on religious tendencies. It probably stems from the embodiment by one of the sexes of some kind of sacred significance which represents a threat to the other. We shall see that, in fact, women thus acquire an isolating power in the eyes of the public which keeps men at a distance not only where sexual relationships are concerned, but in all the minutiae of everyday life. [53]

Although his interpretation of the phenomenon may be questionable, he nonetheless describes very aptly a point we would like to stress: in such communities women represent a negative power and a potential threat, and must therefore be avoided by men. The laws which segregate them are enforced during the whole of their adult lives and cover every aspect of social organization, to which sexual intercourse is only incidental. Men do not necessarily identify with what is sacred, nor women with what is profane; but the use of such categories highlights the tendency – apart from the need to maintain a distinction at all costs – to stress the contrast between superior and inferior beings, and to avoid their intermingling. In fact one section of society has the power to impose its unquestioned authority on the other. Men do their best to discipline women and adolescents, quashing independence and subjecting individuality to the common social cause of which they are the self-imposed guardians. As may be expected, their intervention, whenever possible, is brutal and direct. It can also be purely ideological and indirect when necessary.

Mary Douglas[54] among others[55] has noted that the main purpose of the many taboos concerning uncleanliness is to maintain women in the place society has allotted to them. In communities where the priorities of the sexes are strictly observed sexuality and uncleanliness are rarely associated. Mary Douglas illustrates her observation with examples drawn from Australian Walbiri communities. Here as in all Australian communities the society is based on matrimonial relations. Solidarity is highly developed since living conditions are difficult in this particularly arid region, and all those who are fit to work contribute to the upkeep of the less able. There is a strict hierarchy, adolescents being subjected to their elders and women to men. A woman, once she is married, can no longer count on the protection of her father or her brothers. She is at the mercy of her husband; even her lover, if she has one, will not stand up for her. On the other hand the Walbiri have no taboos as regards menstrual blood.

However there are many primitive societies where the women enjoy a certain degree of freedom and where the weak are protected by law. Even where this is not the case, the means to enforce penalties are not usually available. But as a general rule the importance of the concept of sexual uncleanliness appears to increase in proportion to a society's tolerance. The women are more strictly isolated from the men; they are, in fact, treated somewhat as an inferior caste. Masculinity is often the object of a cult, and in some cases men even go so far as to proclaim their ability to give birth to sons.[56]

Such an attitude is not really surprising when one thinks of the conditions in our enlightened, egalitarian social systems where inequality and segregation reign, enforced by violence and stimulated by possession, and where the whole structure is based on class and racial distinctions. Science, sometimes unwittingly, supports preconceived notions of intellectual and ethical discrepancies between various classes or races, thus enhancing the common Western notion that contact with blacks, paupers, savages or Arabs is not only degrading, but threatens integrity – more or less as primitive societies consider contact with menstrual blood. The implicit purpose of such prejudice is to ensure the domination of one group, by dividing like from unlike or, in other words, superior from inferior beings. This is the natural outcome of a process of institutionalization which sets up visible and invisible barriers to compartmentalize society. There is not and never has been a society where the lowest classes were not more or less excluded and forced to create a society of their own. By attributing specific qualities to women and compelling them to occupy a given place in society men have contrived to reduce them to a similar condition. But on the other hand, as Durkheim observed, such a situation would not have occurred if long-forgotten motives had not led the sexes to separate and to constitute two distinct societies in one; for there is no constitutional basis for such a separation.[57]

2 Men Amongst Themselves

'On the inside that looks like the outside, at the heart of a grip without a grasp, in the passing hours on the margin of the infinite extension of space and time, mouse-trap, man-trap, booby-trap, say, what are you doing? What are you, dark night or the interior of a stone?'

Henri Michaux, *Poteaux d'angle*

(a) Becoming a man

The various customs we have described leave little doubt as to the respective position of each sex, but there is no better example of the non-reciprocity of their relationship than the rites of initiation. Here this non-reciprocity is represented by the child as he is removed from his mother's care and handed over to the father. The situation is very similar to that of the bride in matrimonial transactions who symbolizes the solidarity between males of different clans. It may seem far-fetched to compare initiation and marriage, yet in the social dialogue the common langue of matrimonial laws by which men communicate amongst themselves on the subject of women is paralleled by the esoteric language of male and female non-communication on the subject of children, or rather boys.

Initiation appears to be an almost exclusively male concern. Even when the initiation of girls is practised the ceremonies surrounding the event are always on a more reduced scale than those of their brothers. A boy's initiation signals his admission to the 'hunter's guild' and his physical and technical coming of age. He is henceforth a man, therefore a hunter, and thus all his childhood dreams have come true. Since a woman's duties are less exacting it might seem only natural that the initiation of girls should be non-existent or, at best, less spectacular, but it is difficult not to see in this difference yet another means of stressing their inferiority. As all social and religious activities are reserved exclusively for the initiate, the women are automatically banned and confined to domestic chores from childhood.

To confirm this impression we have only to examine in detail these initiation rites. They invariably involve both physical and intellectual tests. The boys are submitted to painful, humiliating experiences which may even include surgical interventions, in order to prove their endurance and virility. They are segregated from the women, especially from their mothers and sisters, and made aware in every possible way of male authority. Rites celebrating the clan's unity and permanence alternate with rites of passage proper to the occasion. In Terra del Fuego the initiation of girls is restricted to painting them all over and confining them to an isolated hut where they learn the crafts peculiar to women. But the initiation of a boy is the occasion for a complicated ceremony, the *Klo-Koten,* which, besides tests of endurance such as prolonged fasts or lying motionless for twenty-four hours in the snow, involves a procession where the men, disguised as supernatural beings, terrify the women and children, but not the neophyte, who, sworn to secrecy, is informed of the true identify of these creatures. The ceremony ends in a banquet, after which the clan resumes its normal activities.

Among the Yaghan Indians of Chile the neophyte wears ceremonial robes. He has three sponsors and is made to undergo the most demanding tests; he must drink out of a bird's vertebra, scratch himself with a stick and let himself be tattooed; he has also to learn a number of chants and precepts. The ceremony which consists of dancing and singing is followed by a simulated battle between the sexes and then a banquet. Only those who have passed these tests are considered adult, and only those who have passed them twice can attend the mysteries of a further ceremony, the *Kina,* which often follows the initiation rites and whose similarity to the Ona's *Klo-Koten* and to the Alcaley's *Yinchiana* suggests that at some time these different clans must have borrowed from each other.

Initiation frequently involves circumcision. The Wiko of Angola build a hut outside the village precincts for this purpose. It represents the pact concluded between the men and the women to help the adolescent in his progress towards manhood. During the initiation period the youth's parents must abstain from sexual intercourse and the mother renounces her maternal rights in favour of the father with whom the boy now identifies. The generation gap is symbolized in a dance performed by masked men. The boy is thereafter totally separated from his mother whose home he abandons. He is forbidden to associate with her in any way and she must never set eyes on his sexual organs. He has come of age and is ready for marriage and can mingle at all times with the rest of the male community in whose activities he may freely partake. Thus the main purpose of the ritual is to substitute the father and the clan for the mother. Sometimes the process is ritually enacted.

In the rites of initiation the protagonists are the male and female factions and their purpose is to transfer male children from the latter to the former; the plot is sexual antagonism, and the end is masculine supremacy. Robert Jaulin in his moving book *La Mort Sara,*[58] about his own initiation into a Tchad tribe, describes the ceremony as surrounded by the utmost secrecy from its earliest stages when women and other non-initiates are put to flight by a terrifying whistling, throbbing, wailing instrument which also emits groans and moans purporting to be those of long dead ancestors who, at regular intervals, urge their descendants to join the male clan. (In Australia the 'bull-roarer', a stone slab swung round and round at the end of a rope, fulfills the same purpose.) The neophytes are of course in the know, since the deception of women is an essential feature of the ritual, whose purpose is precisely to stress masculine superiority. During initiation the boy is devoured by ancestral spirits, or dies, to be reborn a man, the son of his father. This rebirth is frequently enacted in the form of male parturition; one of the participants seizes the boy and gives birth to him by an age-old magical process stolen from the women. Such rituals would lose all their significance if they were seen and understood by the women. The father's appropriation of his sons is based on the denial of the mother's parturition and the acknowledgement of the father's; this fact must be accepted by the women while the men are accomplices in the deception.

The boy's transfer is the culmination of his initiation and it is both social and physical. Were he to refrain from abandoning his mother he would not be accepted as a member of society, for such an act is tantamount to incest, a crime against the whole tribe. In such an eventuality his sisters would replace him and be transferred in his place from their mother to their father.

On passing the test of manhood the boy enters the circle of the initated where the living inherit the wisdom of their dead. He has learnt the secret language of male communication and the masculine skills and rituals which must never on any account be imparted to the women. For initiation, says Jaulin, celebrates 'man's conquest of himself and of the material and domestic world. Yet the systematic, highly publicized assertion that women have been overcome is partially belied by a certain amount of trickery which suggests that it is not so much a question of dominating the weaker sex as of minimizing their authority to re-establish the balance.'[59]

Thus with the help of a suitable formula the chemistry of social relations enables fathers to give birth to sons by parthenogenesis, or at least to become 'social mothers'. The mothers who are convinced of the ritual's authenticity must pay the stipulated price to buy their sons back if they want to maintain any contact with them.

(b) The duplicity of dominance
Initiation rites reflect the intersection of two spheres. They define the child's sex and prove his manhood while stressing the advantages of being an adult male. For childhood is generally associated with femininity.

When this is not the case, as in Samoa for instance, where the baby boy is removed from his mother's care as soon as he is weaned,[60] there are no initiation rituals.

The true significance of the initiation tests has not been fully grasped. Gregory Bateson writes: 'To some extent, especially in the early stages of initiation (neophytes) play the part of women.'[61] They are teased and humiliated and their initiators, whose sexual organs they are made to handle, call them 'wives'. The ritual involves a kind of exorcism of the female in every male. It imparts a social convention, debasing femininity and exalting masculinity, humiliating the sons of woman to glorify the sons of man in order to preserve the integrity of an all-male clan.

Initiation is the end of innocence: the child has become a man. N. N. Tindale observes that:

The enthusiasm with which young initiates participate in formalities and assimilate the hidden meanings of the mystical traditions and usages of the tribe is quite remarkable. A young man assiduously rehearses the songs and dances of his elders. When he is out hunting with his comrades he undertakes the most dangerous tasks, though he will never forget to retrace his steps in order to remove any tell-tale clue or footprint that might be discovered by a woman, or noticed by one of the elders who would then severely reprimand him.[62]

The realm of manhood has lost its mystery. The secret code that must never on any account be divulged has been revealed. But what is now discovered is not so much the truth as the significance of the law and the distortion of truth. Freedom is for the initiate so long as it remains mysterious and awesome for the others. Knowledge is two-faced, and only through duplicity can the knower maintain the right to be what he is.

However in such matters nothing is ever clear-cut, and the opposing factions of those who know and those who do not are linked together by mutual uncertainty: Are the ignorant really taken in? Do those who know the truth know the whole truth? Secrecy settles the problem without solving it and enforces a convention based on deception and guile. Men are indissolubly bound together as accomplices, and even when they get married their allegiance is to other men on whom their authority and manhood depend. The young man resolutely turns to his like in an effort to stress the contrast, prove his new allegiance and reject that which, to his shame, is still part of him.

On the other hand initiation rites penetrate the sphere of male and female antagonism, where sons are the bone of contention. According to Roheim: 'The purpose of all initiation rites is to remove sons from their mothers so that they can be integrated into their father's clan.'[63] Instead of finding aid and support in their growing sons mothers must give them up and get nothing in return. It is probably because primitive peoples realized the unfairness of such a custom that they enshrined it in a justificatory mythology. Individuals and society had to be gradually conditioned to accept it. Conflicts are ritually enacted to exorcize the threat of an ever-deferred disaster – woman's revolt against masculine authority and prerogatives. Undoubtedly the frenzy of the rituals celebrates a renewed victory over a perennial enemy, and initiation itself is only another aspect of woman's subjection to man, no different in this respect from the segregation of habitat and diet.

Hence men and women become two distinct social categories, especially when structure and kinship are relatively fluid, as with the Hadza hunting tribes. 'Wherever Hadza are, and whatever they do, they are always controlled by the division between the sexes. This division is between two hostile classes, each of which is capable of organizing itself for defence or virulent attack against the other. This extraordinarily intense consciousness of sexual difference is the only permanent level of organization the Hadza ever achieve,' writes Mary Douglas. [64]

But in reality, with a few rare exceptions, this difference permeates the social and technical activity of all peoples, leaving its mark on language, behaviour, ideals, rituals, living and working conditions, and even sexual relations where frigidity is woman's only means of achieving freedom by non-acceptance, or at least by non-participation, while the men endeavour to rekindle the flame they have extinguished. Similarly the much prized virility of the men proves that they are the masters and that the women they have conquered are only there to honour and accept them. Should these attitudes be modified, as they have recently been in Africa, and woman assert her independence, then the sexual balance is affected. Robert Le Vine reports such an occurrence among the Yoruba, where male impotence – actual among certain men and dreaded by the rest – has become a constant preoccupation, while rituals and customs tend to require female disguises: 'These fragments of disparate evidence suggest that among the Yoruba the alteration of traditional sex roles has reached the stage where men are not simply resentful of female independence but feel emasculated and envy it.' [65]

Revealing as such an attitude may be as regards present-day problems in relations between the sexes, it also throws some light on the past. If woman came to be seen as an object and a sign in kinship societies this was the result of a deliberate effort on the part of such societies – an effort which can be detected in our contemporary structures. Since this object and sign was also a being of flesh and blood capable of resisting her oppressors and of piercing, at any moment, the veil of mystery and duplicity which protected them, the precariousness of the situation must frequently have assumed the dimension of a threat to masculine dominance and thus to law and order in general. The continued reassertion of social conventions and the partiality of initiation served to dissipate such a threat and to maintain law and order. Behind the so-called natural difference which turned one of the sexes into a commodity and the other into its traders, emerges the struggle of the sexes which has influenced humanity biologically, psychologically and historically in so many different but unmistakable ways.

The existence of this sexual conflict in primitive societies dispels the myth of their presumed simplicity and uniformity. Simultaneously it makes them appear less 'foreign'; alive and involved in the effort of self-generation rather than reacting solely to biological and environmental requirements with survival as their only objective. One cannot deny the relation between the prohibition of incest from which all other prohibitions stem, and the struggle of the sexes. This relation is revealed in the parallel between the true motivation of the prohibition and the social distinction between men and women. But we have still to discover what made such regulations necessary and what they signify.

[x]

Part Nature, Part Culture

1 *A Basic Distinction*

(a) *Two general phenomena*

There are two phenomena which are common to all human societies: The prohibition of incest and the distinction between male and female occupations.[66] This coincidence is not fortuitious and it could throw some light on the struggle between the sexes and the laws which enforce the hierarchical relations between them. Marcel Mauss observed half a century ago: 'Classification by sex is a basic classification whose impact on society is greater than we suspect. Our social sciences are sadly below par in this respect. We ought to confess to our students, especially to those who are preparing to do field work, that we have only studied male sociology, and not female sociology or the sociology of the two sexes in their relations to each other.' [67] Things have not changed very much since those days. Women are still an unexplored sphere, a sideline of knowledge; they exist in reality but not in theory.

Less than two centuries ago historians observed a similar attitude towards the working classes: history was only concerned with kings and noblemen. When the voice of the people was finally heard proclaiming their social rights, history began to include the masses among its protagonists and the social sciences made an effort to understand them. Mauss's remark may help to demonstrate the fact that women, as objects of social exchange, are also the terms of such an exchange, and thus enable us to understand the significance of the above-mentioned coincidence. But first let us return briefly to natural division and affiliation societies.

The primitive family combines a social unit and a productive unit. It unites two individuals for whom such a union is licit, and whose skills and aptitudes are complementary. Prohibition and exogamy account for the first unit, which was the only one that appeared to require an explanation. The productive unit and the distinction from which it stems seemed natural since the division of labour according to sex is supposed to correspond to natural, biological distinctions. It needed no further justification; and this for two reasons. First, production and all the technical and material aspects of civilization are seen as secondary, and not worthy of being institutionalized. On the other hand, the biological nature of the male and female division of labour made its institutionalization superfluous. Thus the prohibition of incest is only concerned with blood relationships (by defining permitted and prohibited marriages), and not with the differences between male and female skills and aptitudes. In other words, the reciprocity between men that is concretized in matrimonial alliances is taken to be a *social* rule; but the male dominance of females and the differentiation of their social activities, are taken to be natural phenomena, already regulated by nature, and requiring no further social rule. The concordance between the two general social phenomena mentioned above has been overlooked.

The division of pursuits according to sex is seen as the rational outcome of objective physiological circumstances: maternity and child care naturally devolve to women and not to men, so communal existence is neatly divided between the former who assume the household chores and the latter who assume the important social responsibilities. Robin Fox writes:

> For the greater part of human history woman's role was restricted to bearing and bringing up children. It was the men who hunted, fought and ruled. I am convinced that this division is rooted in primate constitution and that, although in our relatively recent past social conditions in certain advanced societies have enabled women to have their say, most of them will accept my verdict ... because the purely physical aspect of childbearing confines women to a secondary role with respect to men in all matters outside the household sphere. [68]

But apart from actual childbearing and the female physical constitution which, it is said, preclude women from participating fully and equally in communal activities, their specific psychological and physiological disposition is supposed to restrict the range of their productive occupations. For instance: 'Women have a capacity for continuous monotonous work, that men do not share, while men have a capacity for the mobilization of sudden spurts of energy followed by a need for rest and reassemblage of resources,' according to Margaret Mead. [69] G. P. Murdock asserts that:

> By virtue of their primary sex differences, a man and a woman make an exceptionally efficient cooperating unit. Man, with his superior physical strength, can better undertake the more strenuous tasks. ... Not handicapped, as is woman, by the physiological burdens of pregnancy and nursing, he can range farther afield to hunt, to fish, to herd and to

trade. Woman is at no disadvantage, however, in lighter tasks which can be performed in or near the home. .... All known human societies have developed specialization and cooperation between the sexes roughly along this biologically determined line of cleavage.[70]

And for Emile Durkheim, this division was part of a general cleavage which gradually induced feminine docility and fragility, in fact all the specific psychological, anatomical and neurological characteristics of the sex.[71]

The inferiority of women is logically deduced from their circumstances. The sequence of determining factors is obvious: biological bimorphism gives rise to a division of communal, productive activities and the different importance ascribed to such activities has influenced the respective status of the sexes. An economist estimated that the status of women was inferior to that of men in 87 per cent of the pastoral communities he observed, but in agricultural communities the ratio was reduced to 73 per cent. According to him the discrepancy is due to the fact that men are better fitted for the more specialized task of tending flocks, whereas women can, if necessary, master the art of cultivating the land.

Obviously there is no need for social laws to enforce such natural, genetically determined distinctions. This conclusion, though not always explicitly stated, is taken for granted and its social implications are never questioned. Scientists — seemingly on the most objective grounds — tend to agree with the Marquis de Sade who declared:

What do I observe when I pursue my inquiry in cold blood? A puny creature, in every way man's inferior, infinitely less beautiful, less clever and less wise than he, repulsively constituted ... in brief an evil, outlandish being as different from man as man is different from the apes of the woods and whose pretensions to humanity were very seriously questioned during several sittings of the Council of Mâcon.[72]

However combined ethnographic and historical evidence reveals that women, notwithstanding their presumed biological handicaps, have in fact generally participated fully in communal activities, undertaking and carrying out essential tasks. It is only in the relatively well-to-do, unproductive, strata of society that their role is seen as restricted to the producing of heirs. In fact devices such as infanticide, abortion and birth control reflect the need for the participation of women in social labour. Furthermore the tasks allotted to men and to women vary from one culture to another. In North America tanning is a woman's job while in the south west it is a man's. In Arizona the Hopi men spin and weave while the neighbouring Navaho allot such tasks to their women; similarly, according to Herodotus, spinning and weaving was done by the men in

Egypt and by the women in Greece. Bantu women are not allowed to tend the flocks, but Hottentot women do the milking. Nonetheless in all cases there is a differentiation between male and female activities, and the latter are invariably taken to be inferior, in that they are avoided by men even when they are technically very similar to male occupations.

Yet such distinctions obviously do not correspond to sexual bimorphism. Moreover physical and anatomical differences cannot account for the fact that in so many societies women are not only forbidden to hunt, but are not even allowed to handle the weapons and implements used by the men. Since the common excuse that this attitude shows natural masculine chivalry and paternal solicitude is highly questionable, one can only assume that such prohibitions really have the function of creating distinctions that will consolidate a wholly artificial (i.e. non-biological) differentiation. The hierarchical difference between male and female is not the result of the division of labour, nor can it be attributed to biological causes. It is the pre-established social hierarchy which is reflected in the assumed dignity or indignity of occupations and which conditions their division. Such a division is not the result of individual or family decisions but of a general social competition and separation. It refers us to general forms of social organization which have recurred throughout history. It is completely unrealistic to see the family as a social phenomenon and the division of labour as a purely natural one.

(b) Sex before class

Since the division of labour according to sex cannot be explained physiologically, it might perhaps be considered in the light of a more general development such as natural division. Our inquiry is restricted to a single period, admittedly the longest in the history of mankind, when as a consequence of changes involving resources, demography, organic and inorganic faculties and environmental relationships, the males of the species became hunters and the females continued to collect and gather. But for such changes sexual dichotomy would probably not have occurred. J. H. Steward says: 'As far as we know the process of gathering food does not promote a sexual division of labour since both sexes employ the same methods.'[73] The division of skills and implements results neither from innate aptitudes, choice nor mutual agreement, but from the sequence of changes in which both sexes were involved. The diversity of their pursuits corresponded to the requirements of the community in a specific environment; like all such divisions, it was the solution to a general problem.[74] The strict separation of hunters from gatherers was a *sine qua non* for the process of adapting specific skills to a specific environment, for ensuring the transmission of such skills and for maintaining a close relationship with this environment which was animal for one group and vegetable for the other. In the course of such natural divisions the new group, or natural category, invariably tends to see its particular world as the only world, or at least as the yardstick by which the rest of the world is measured. Its skills, knowledge and beliefs represent all that it is possible to achieve, know and believe, and barriers of all kinds must be erected to safeguard the hard core of reality, which is the group's prerogative, against the misguided ignorance of outsiders. The hunter looks down on the gatherer, and in turn the cultivator looks down on the hunter, the craftsman on the cultivator, the builder on the craftsman and so on.

This conflict between hunter, shepherd or cultivator figures in all mythologies and religions, from Abel the shepherd murdered by the cultivator Cain, onwards. It reflects the desire to preserve the integrity of a traditional pursuit and the rivalry between old and new methods of production. But there is generally a period of transition when the new category is still marginal. In some African tribes the blacksmith and the carpenter are not allowed within the village precincts and are forbidden to cultivate the soil. Since they are compelled to beg for the corn they cannot grow they are likened to scavengers and nicknamed the Fox or the Hyena.[75] But no sooner have such craftsmen asserted their rights than they become, as in Ancient Greece, symbols of intelligence and thought.

As symptoms and as means antagonism, separation and hierarchy further the cause of natural division. But Engels aptly observed that the division of labour between the sexes is conditioned by factors other than the position of women in society.'[76] Society adapts each successive division to its own ends, and primarily to that of sexual discrimination. For although man's domination of woman is not genetically motivated[77] it is already a feature of affiliation societies. In these it only refers to sexual and hierarchical relations. There is little diversity in the activities, aptitudes and environmental relationships of the sexes, though the males are usually responsible for the protection of communities and territories. It is only with the specialization of hunting and gathering that differentiation extends to skills and activities. But male dominance is at the same time restricted by their dependence on females, since the very fact of male specialization in one field establishes the women as specialized in another no less important field. In such circumstances collaboration is inevitable. On the other hand the segregation of reproductive and non-reproductive males in primate and hominid societies left its mark on the whole social structure, but mainly on the interrelationship of different male generations. The tensions which characterized such relationships were presumably transferred to heterosexual relations when hunting made intergeneration collaboration necessary.

A relevant feature of affiliation societies is the link albeit very tenuous — which persists between mothers and sons after these youngsters have been banished to the periphery and which becomes their only remaining connection with the community. As hunting developed the advantage of having large, well-organized bands incited the adult males to recruit these youngsters and separate them from their mothers. With the diversification of aptitudes and fields of activity young males became a new and significant asset which the men promptly appropriated thanks to the social prerogatives they already enjoyed. The male group was forced to come to terms with the relatively independent female group while keeping it under strict control. For in such communities social government is direct and personal, hierarchy is based on individual participation in essential communal activities and objects are identified as persons; in our social structures, on the contrary, social government is concerned with objects, hierarchy is based on ownership and individuals become identified as objects.

It is not unreasonable to assume that the division between hunters and gatherers first occurred within the framework of a hierarchy of participation where considerable discrepancies in ranking order spread through the whole structure. Malinowski writes: 'The division of labour is rooted in the brutal subjection of the weaker sex to the stronger.'[78] And this first division predetermined those which followed. It may be inferred that man's dependence on female cooperation in production and on the relinquishing of the females' rights to their male children persisted and influenced social behaviour in general, promoting apposite laws and regulations. This seems all the more probable since the relationship between social categories was also a relationship between productive categories, at least until property became a reality reflected in the opposing factions of exploiters and workers. At the time an individual's social rank was determined by his occupation. Humanity consisted mainly of hunters, gatherers, cultivators or shepherds, each category belonging to a particular clan, tribe, sex or age group and possessing distinctive biological and psychological characteristics; i.e. each category had a social status with associated rights and duties. As Lévi-Strauss says, 'whether considered from the point of view of caste or totemic clan it must be admitted that the allocation of social functions corresponds to the division of natural spheres – or that the world of beings corresponds to that of things.'[79]

Social categories are identified with natural categories; and when these refer to one or other of the sexes the dual process of socialization and naturalization increases the discrepancies which social existence and evolution had already established. The division becomes a general phenomenon dividing the whole universe into male and female. Our myths and our legends reflect and perpetuate it in a form which, even if we do not take it literally, we cannot dismiss as pure fiction and unrelated to man's vision of reality.[80]

With the emergence of class societies a radical change occurs. Indirect economic and political systems replace direct systems, while a class distinction and a structure based on property replace those based on male and female participation. The distinction between possessors and dispossessed determines all other relationships. Where aptitudes, skills and those who exercised them (Marc Bloch's 'invention carriers') had been classified according to sex, they are now classified according to a no less organic criterion involving and opposing the hand and the brain – or manual and intellectual labour – with no possible doubt as to which is superior. The male and female principles which had governed man and the world are rejected for the dichotomy between mind and matter. But apart from this the means of expressing social differences, oppositions and disparities have not changed. When we are exhorted to take up arms against natural instincts we are really being enlisted as one human category against another and against instincts we refuse to recognize as our own.

This division has its own peculiar dynamic which varies with the structure of the society – a dynamic frequently misinterpreted by scientists who ascribe it to specific physical and anatomical causes and confuse its effects with those of genetic processes, notably where the forms of female subjection peculiar to primitive societies are concerned. To refer to it as an appropriation of women by men as Engels has done, or to compare it to the ranking order and dominance proper to primate societies as ethnologists and anthropologists tend to do, is to reduce the division of labour and the relation between the sexes to the level of technical, economic or irrational and instinctive phenomena. When the inequality of the sexes is attributed to bimorphism or to biological necessity the struggle for egalitarianism becomes useless. It is only by stressing the weakness of such arguments that the struggle acquires its true historical and current significance. Moreover this struggle results from the combined effects of division, understood as a general phenomenon, and of the social and economic institutions which ensure male dominance. These account for woman's subjection without resorting to hypothetical constructions such as promiscuity, maternal responsibilities, different male and female brain structures, primate genetics, a shortage of women or the physical and intellectual shortcomings of the weaker sex. It also accounts for the fact that societies gradually adopted a law or convention – the prohibition of incest – which is associated with the polymorphism of the struggle in every sphere.

2 *The Prohibition of Incest: Its Role in Exogamy and in Natural Division*

The prohobition of incest tallied with the social structure men had created for themselves during this extended period when men and women were strictly divided in their activities, implements and aptitudes. Intermingling was reduced to a minimum and each category was associated with the sphere of reality to which it was restricted by laws which established the boundaries of its material and intellectual horizon. Their independence was subjected to an ever-renewed interdependence: responsibilities were shared, displacements organized, and their activities obeyed annual seasonal rhythms. Status and pursuits however, were determined at birth according to sex. As E. Evans-Pritchard writes:

> It is perhaps sufficient to draw attention to one major difference; that of the mother-son and of the father-daughter relationships. As soon as a boy has grown out of childhood he comes under the sole authority of his father, and the mother ceases to have any say in his ubpringing and exercises very little influence over him. On the other hand, a girl comes under the almost exclusive control of her mother, and, beyond arranging her marrige, her father takes little interest in her affairs. [81]

Since such a division of responsibilities corresponds to no biological imperative, girls and boys have to be conditioned in their respective allegiances from early childhood. F. W. Young writes: 'In as much as societies have a sexual division of labour and some form of marriage, a well defined sex role becomes functionally necessary when the boy nears the threshold of participation in such social patterning.'[82] The dividing line between male and female must be respected in every sphere of social relationship and activity.

Separating sons from their mothers is a specific aspect of such a division. Once the cooperation of youngsters had become an asset the men had to find a means of appropriating them. They had to find a plausible motive for prohibiting any further bond between these potential collaborators and their mothers. In affiliation societies the autonomy of reproductive and mother-son units automatically precluded such an eventuality. But when both units merged into a single family unit incest became not only possible but a means of consolidating this unit and abstracting it from the community. To avoid such a danger while maintaining parental relations with their sons, the men contrived to make the estrangement of mothers and sons a preliminary condition for initiation. When property, money and secular power came into their own the ritual persisted, though the institution became redundant. It was replaced by the law of nature which, as Hobbes says:

> requires that the victor should be lord and master over the vanquished. Whence it follows that a child is under the immediate tutelage of parent who is first responsible for it. However, it so happens that the mother is responsible for her new born child before anybody else, so that she is able to bring it up or expose it, at her own free will without referring to any other authority. If by marriage contract women undertake to live under their husbands' control, their common offspring

will be under paternal control on account of this same control being already over their mother.[83]

Some writers have given considerable prominence to a presumed conflict in primitive societies between fathers and sons for the possession of women. It would be nearer the truth to say that all primitive societies are based on the struggle between fathers and mothers for the possession of sons. A lot of rituals have no other motive. 'It is equally obvious,' says Roheim, 'that it is the father who separates sons and mothers and that such a separation is motivated by the Oedipus complex.'[84] Unless, of course, it is more plausible to suggest that separation and those causes which gave rise to it were themselves the origin of the Oedipal conflict as a psychological structure elaborated and transmitted through successive generations.

Differences in male and female hierarchial status spread to all fields of social activity. But within the family they encounter a potential stumbling block. For if a man were to marry his own sister, daughter or mother he could no longer treat her as chattel since parental and conjugal bonds conflict. By making her his wife he raises her status and his own decreases in proportion. However the prohibition of incest solves the problem of this dual necessity of separation and hierarchy. It creates a barrier between the sexes. Relations between parents and children of opposite sexes or between brothers and sisters involve distinctions inherent in each sex. Girls and boys are shunted into their respective, unequal tracks to forestall the development of stable relationships.

If the prohibition lays particular stress on the mother-son relationship it is because boys are required to cooperate in their father's undertakings while remaining within the family circle. The precariousness of such a situation and the risk of social roles becoming confused is diminished when the boy joins the adult male group and experiences the rebirth of initiation. A number of primitive peoples seem to make no connection between sexual intercourse and conception; but what is generally seen as downright ignorance might well be a wilful refusal to acknowledge a connection which could only be detrimental to paternal possession by exposing the impossibility of male parthenogenesis. Initiation rites confirm the separation between mothers and sons, since the youth who comes of age and is officially promoted from one age group to another really celebrates his passage from an inferior to a superior sex and rank.

By forbidding marriages between members of a clan or family, the prohibition of incest removes the obstacle to the establishment of a hierarchy within the clan or family. The brides who are selected from different, possibly enemy, clans are foreign and thus inferior by definition. Lee and De Vore write: 'With regard to the question of the "hunter's mentality" the Ona [of Tierra del Fuego] are particularly instructive.

There were a number of ingenious institutions which were effective in minimising intra-band hostilities and in channelling aggression toward outsiders or towards wives, who, in strictness, were outsiders.'[85] As outsiders, wives can be treated as menials without infringing the laws of clan hierarchy. When a man gives away his own daughters and sisters he is indirectly and through the medium of another clan treating them as inferiors, which he could not do to his own daughters and sisters. (Such a possibility is not entirely ruled out but it conflicts with other necessities, of cooperation and so on). Thus through the transfer of women each sex and age group finds its appropriate rank.

Theoretically at least the women of one clan are always natives of another and each clan is composed of two socially distinct halves. Birdsell observes: 'The woman's position there is such that she has little chance to influence language, ceremony or male functions in the total culture. These imported wives are silent nonentities until they learn the language of their husband's group, and then they are quickly absorbed into the husband's band and tribe.'[86] Language, our man instrument of communication, is also an instrument of non-communication and dissociation. The profusion of dialects, syntaxes, semantic fields, signs and double or triple entendres corresponds to a desire for secrecy, or a desire to incorporate the incomprehensible and the particular into the comprehensible and the general. Fluency in a secret or unknown language is a tremendous asset and a powerful means of intimidating those who have not mastered it. Similarly religions, myths, philosophy and science which all endeavour to extract meaning from chaos, to relate cause and effect, and to make the unintelligible intelligible, in fact also reduce significance to chaos, isolate cause and effect and surround light with a zone of darkness. Thought indicates by obliterating and constructs by concealing. Those who are caught in the whirlpool of crosscurrents have only a vague premonition of the still centre of significance beneath the swirling unfamiliarity of words and references. Excluded and diminished they learn subjection.

Because of the tender age at which girls are given away in marriage, a clan rarely includes adult females who are not of foreign extraction and who can rely on the protection of a blood relation. Marriage, which for a young man is a short cut to authority, power and responsibility, reduces a girl's status and restricts her to the world of household chores which was her mother's before her. The woman from whom a man purloins his male child is really an outsider who has no one to stand up for her and whose isolation and subjection are increased by this added deprivation; this occasion which celebrates masculine alliance in the admission of a new member to its ranks, simultaneously stresses her estrangement. Marriage, as Geroge Davy says, is inseparable from 'the sex struggle and consequently from family and tribal feuds'.[87] The fact that it is inseparable from the prohibition of incest indicates the social significance of the prohibition.

For the prohibition is a product of society, and it refers to natural and to social bonds. Its main purpose is to encourage the autonomy and responsibility of each sex in their appropriate fields of action. Within the limits of family, clan or tribal organization it maintains the stability of the material order on which society is built. Its impact on the distribution of individuals, aptitudes and property ensures the continuity of a given environment by specifying the responsibility and sphere of activity proper to each group. Furthermore by promoting this division it has gradually adapted it to the general outline of social structure, that is to say to male dominance. And here its true purpose comes to light. For the prohibition has been truly effective and indispensable where human relationships with the environment are concerned; the regulation of sexual partnerships is only a secondary aspect. As the social expression of a natural division it is the process which enabled communities already split into gatherers and hunters to enforce adequate laws for their growth and development. Moreover it gave a human significance to sexual relations.

Through its impact the family as productive unit became a social element in the general collective stysem. Then inequality and conflict became general and unilateral dependence replaced cooperation. Exogamic division was adapted to a hierarchy of participation and later to a hierarchy of appropriation purporting to be exchanged, in which the men, as usual, asserted their rights and prerogatives over the women. The laws of kinship enforced by the men regulated the alliances which ensured them permanent ascendancy over their imported brides.

The division resulting from the prohibition of incest reflects the natural tendency to distribute the members of a society between the various compartments of reality, knowledge and labour as well as to curb instincts and encourage conventional behaviour. It further reflects the exogamic tendency to unite social groups by directing parental authority towards precise sexual ends. In this respect it expresses simultaneously a very ancient tradition – that is male dominance – and the emergence of a new attitude as the scene and conventions of sexual relationships began to change.

[XI]

In Praise of Discipline

1 Incest, Arch-enemy of Civilization

(A) The primal fear

Human discipline is a tribute to the prohibition of incest, that insurmoutable barrier safeguarding the interests of society against animal instinct and chaos. Georges Bataille writes: 'There is something in the horror of incest which stresses our humanity, and the problem it poses can be seen as the problem of mankind in so far as it adds a human dimension to animal nature.'[88] Incest represents unruliness, social discord and rivalry between fathers and sons for the possession of women. It portends a return to nature, the abolition of distinctions, the transgression of laws and can only lead to the just retributions such crimes deserve.

Now I am compelled, in order to be consistent with the ideas I have hitherto advanced, to challenge this notion of the natural horror incest inspires. At no time have I suggested the possibility of an original state of non-differentiation, of aleatory sexual relations or of regular incestuous habits. Nor have I assumed that the prohibition was the answer to an actual or potential state of disorderliness. I cannot therefore explain it as being the result of such real or imaginary conditions. Should it then be inferred that this horror is unmotivated? Freud declared that we do not know the origins of incest and do not even know where to look for them.[89] The only clue we have is the prohibition itself. It operates through separation and through hierarchy. First it separates the sexes by isolating them in their different activities (initiation serves as a means of stressing the separation of sons from their mothers); and it further establishes a definite hierarchy between them. Incest must be considered in the context of male and female groups, and not, as hitherto, in an exclusively male context. The prohibition then emerges as a means of consolidating hierarchical distinctions, and as motivated by the fear of an anticipated rather than a remembered danger. Its function is not to protect against an ancient danger but to prevent an eventuality which is always possible – a reaction against an organization of society which ensures male dominance.

Its purpose is not to organize sexual unions, nor to transform a biological into a social unit. Promiscuity was never a feature of our past history, nor does it threaten our future; therefore it does not require repression. The true nature of our horror of incest can be explained by the fact that the prohibition is simply one among the many prejudices or written and unwritten laws which tend to perpetuate social discrimination. [90] Such laws were never created to eradicate actual laxness. Racial prejudice against the blacks in North America began when slavery began; the poor were segregated from the rich because it was decreed that the gulf between them was unbridgeable; manual labourers were despised because of the arbitrary assumption that manual labour was inferior to intellectual labour. Distinctions and inequality come first; colour, district, dialect or trade are then used as pretexts to justify prejudice and to give it an appearance of logic. They are symbols used to divide the world into right and wrong, high and low, human and non-human. The laws of segregation may at times be overlooked in private, but never in public, matters. Wherever status derives from race, class or profession an infringement of the law constitutes a danger which must be avoided at all cost. Yet the dichotomy — accepted by those if favours as well as by those it deprives — is fundamentally reversible.

We live in fear because we know that an order based on repression, elitism and constraint contains the seeds of revolt. At all times masters have been haunted by the terror of one day seeing servants refuse to obey. For such a refusal is said to herald the end of society and progress. And incest is the rust which starts to corrode 'the ladder of degree', to open the way to anarchy and the 'confusion of relations' (the literal translation of the Chinese ideogram for incest[91]), and which levels out distinctions, producing legendary monsters. It is a weapon in the hands of women who will disrupt man-made order, retain their sons and assert their equality. It may not be their only weapon but it is the most generally dreaded.

(b) Oedipus and Antigone

The implications of this dread are nowhere better expressed than in the tragedy of Oedipus, where its progress is summed up in the solving of two riddles with diametrically opposed consequences. The first riddle is asked by the Sphinx who obstructs the way to Thebes and to incest. To accept this strange creature's challenge is to accept its definition of man as distinct from animal and from woman. And it becomes obvious that the purpose of its riddles is to make sure that the preliminary conditions for incest should be established; incest is only possible and significant — the tragedy itself makes this clear — when it is the act of a social human being. But Oedipus, having solved the first riddle, proceeds on his way to the city where he will be king.

The second riddle is that of his birth. The calamities which have descended on Thebes require that a scapegoat should be found. Someone must be responsible, and all the clues point inexorably to Oedipus who, forced to delve into his past, discovers his real identity and how he has unwittingly brought a curse upon his subjects. He learns what everybody else already seemed to know: that he has murdered Laisu his father and married his mother Jocasta.

Freud asserts that these two crimes result from a son's incestuous desire for his mother and the consequent rivalry between father and son — two exclusively male circumstances. But desire and rivalry are far from prominent in the tragedy of which the parents' antagonism forms the hub. Laius, who has been told that his son will murder him and then marry his widow, tries to forestall this fate by ordering the death of the infant Oedipus. But Jocasta, opposing male authority, contrives to save the child's life. This act of rebellion simultaneously asserts her own power and brings the downfall of her husband. Their conflicting aims require that each should use the child against the other. Laius knows that the survival of a son he does not entirely dominate will enable Jocasta to assume authority, and Jocasta knows that by saving her son she will destroy Laius. Oedipus marries Jocasta in all innocence. For him this union represents only fatherhood and kingship. For those who know the terrible secret, it is incest. The main culprit is, of course, Jocasta whose insubordination made it possible in the first place and who later, when the truth is about to be revealed, tries to dissuade Oedipus from delving further into the past. She would rather he were blind, that he should accomplish his fate in blindness; and blindness is the accomplishment of his fate. Jocasta plays an active part. The whole action takes place between mother and father, not between mother and son. She is responsible for the disasters which befalls the city, for it is she who infringed the rule of male domination, and she will pay the heaviest penalty.

There are two two significant points to this tragedy. The first is the abortive murder of the son by his father — Laius is a criminal without a crime. This has obvious initiation connotations. In the rites of passage the neophyte's symbolic death is a prelude to his rebirth as an adult and as the son of his father; if he were not initiated he would remain under his mother's authority and be lost to the father. These rituals where life and death are joined revive the eternal antagonism between male and female by ratifying the latter's subjection and by stressing the precariousness of the former's authority. The child is both stake and mediator in a contest which involves his own existence and in which his parents ruthlessly pursue their own ends, each seeing him only as a weapon against the other. In such conditions he is certainly more likely to feel terror than desire or rivalry for his parents.

The second point is that Jocasta's successful though secret rebellion against her husband's authority occasions the downfall of both parents.

Laius attempts to forestall the incestuous act that threatens his authority and his life, while Jocasta is the agent of its accomplishment. Oedipus kills his father and fulfils the prediction of the oracle, but he is only an instrument. Jocasta has chosen her fate and cannot ignore the fatal consequences of her choice; she dies by Oedipus's hand but as a result of her own actions. Insubordination is the crime of crimes and entails capital punishment. It is woman's sole weapon against man's tyranny, but it is self-defeating. Oedipus who survives is not alone responsible for the calamity which occurred, for: 'on man and wife falls mingled punishment.'[92]

This reading of the tragedy reveals the prohibition as separation. By solving the Sphinx's riddle Oedipus repudiated the world of women. Then he delves into his past and is initiated when he discovers the struggle which had taken place for his possession. He is a man among men. The prohibition of incest concerns the mother's possession of her son, not the son's of his mother.

But the tragedy itself starts after incest has been committed and it stresses the hierarchical aspect of the prohibition. Incest appears as woman's endeavour to revrse a hierarchy that disfavours her. Since Jocasta has succeeded in saving Oedipus from the fate to which his father had condemned him and in destroying her husband and marrying her son, she has established her daughters in the line of succession instead of their brothers. Oedipus exclaims

What then? They ape Egyptian manners, do they? Where men keep house and do embroidery while wives go out to earn the daily bread? Insread of troubling themselves about my business, they sit at home like girls and let you two bear all the burden of my calamities.' [93]

A Bushong myth throws further light on the significance of this reversal. Woot, the first ancestor, sprawls naked, overcome by drink, and is mocked by his sons while his daughters dutifully cover his nakedness. When he awakes and learns what has happened he banishes his sons, forcing them to undergo long and painful initiation tests, while his daughters become his heirs. Is Oedipus's rejection of his sons and election of his daughters a consequence of the transgression he has been led to commit? The author of the tragedy leaves this question unanswered.

But what he does make quite clear is the danger of anarchy, that women may question their masters' decision or even go so far as to make decisions themselves. Jocasta achieves her ends by guile and subterfuge, but her daughter Antigone, in the tragedy which bears her name, acts entirely in the open. Here we are left in no doubt as to the choices made, the object of contention and the price that has to be paid: she opposes the rule of man without ambiguity. Her uncle King creon observes:

There is no more deadly peril than disobediance: States are devoured
by it, homes laid in ruins, Armies defeated, victory turned to rout,
While simple obediance saves the lives of hundreds of honest folk.
Therefore, I hold to the law, and will never betray it – least of all for a
woman. Better be beaten, if need be, by a man, than let a woman get
the better of us.'[94]

The consequences of anarchy could not be more clearly specified.
Antigone is a woman who refuses to obey, and openly opposes man. The
docility of her sister Ismene highlights her inflexibility: 'O think,
Antigone; we are women; it is not for us to fight against men; our rulers
are stronger than we, and we must obey in this, or in worse than this.' [95]
Later Antigone counters this statement with: 'Life was your choice, when
mine was death.' [96] Life equals submission; revolt can only lead to certain
defeat and to death. Antigone would substitute for the man-made rule of
the city a rule of brotherly duty; she incurs thus Creon's fury. The king is
even prepared to face the death of his own son, Antigone's betrothed, of
whom he says: 'Despicable coward! No more will than a woman!' [97] At
the climax of the tragedy he declares: 'Go then, and share your love
among the dead. We'll have no woman's law here, while I live.' [98] A law
furthermore, which is an infringement of the prohibition, since Antigone's
burial of her brother Polynices is a symbolic incest and therefore cannot be
tolerated by Creon.

Creon, the opponent of anarchy and upholder of the law, kills his own
son for submitting to a woman's will. The circle is closed; we are back
where we started though in reverse, since the first action was that of
Oedipus, victim of another woman's scheme, murdering his own father. In
the natural sphere of predictable fate incest is the outcome of male and
female inequality and of their struggle for the possession of their son. In
the social sphere the right which one of the sexes claims to rule over and
dictate to the other provokes rebellion and unrest. Jocasta working in the
dark and Antigone unafraid in the open both challenge the laws of man.
They evoke the ever-present threat of incest with its inevitable aftermath,
the 'shaking of degrees'. And this is what Laius and Creon both dread, the
former dimly, the latter quite distinctly. However the disaster which they
really seek to avoid at all costs is not a return to nature and chaos but the
equality and freedom of women. But woman's struggle is doomed to
failure from the start; the scales are too unevenly weighted. Antigone is
entombed alive with the dead, still proclaiming her rights, while Jocasta
succumbs to her secret defiance. Only law-abiding Ismene survives.

In these tragedies the city centres around the arena where children are
the stake, men and women the contenders, and the prohibition of incest
the rule of the game; a rule enforced by the organizing faction which
condemns any initiative from those who are not its members, opposes

spontaneous personal inclinations and only allows the submissive to survive. Transgression spells anarchy and disaster because it would change the course of events and alter the respective positions of the factions involved.

Seen in this light the prohibition, far from abolishing a primitive state of unruliness and chaos, creates a perpetual state of potential disorder in that it accumulates repressive violence; by reinforcing the differentiation of the sexes and precluding egalitarianism, it promotes rebellion and ultimately chaos. That section of society which it condemns to function as objects and symbols must oppose it in order simply to live and to survive. However if the way of rebellion is pursued long enough it should lead, through chaos, to a new order where each individual will be entitled to his own share of happiness, power, equality and culture. Incest – in certain societies the privilege of an elite – is a token of such a rebellion, the abolition of a prohibition in favour of a new order. It is dreaded because it is associated to some extent with the legendary Reign of Women. According to Lévi-Strauss: woman's social insubordination, frequently alluded to in myths, foreshadows in the image of the 'reign of women', an infinitely worse peril: that of her physiological insubordination. Therefore women must be *regulated;* their physiological peculiarity thus being made to prove the connection between social and natural rhythms and to vindicate a subjection instilled by education and enforced by a man-made, inequitable society.[99] The dread which the possibility of such a reign inspires proves that all the measures taken to prevent it stem from male dominance and are a means of maintaining law and order by violence. My theory eliminates the hypothesis of natural promiscuity and makes it quite clear that the struggle of the sexes results from discrimination and hierarchy.

Social order is not the only sign – nor indeed the sole purpose – of culture. That which is forbidden is equally significant. Prohibitions divide the familiar and the communicable from what must be maintained in mystery and not communicated. Transgression enables the ignorant to acquire knowledge, slaves to become masters and disorder to initiate a new order.

2 *The Eternal Present*

The significance and the function of the prohibition of incest have been modified with the passing of time. In its original context the prohibition had a negative and a positive connotation; it stood for alliance (between men) and exclusion (of women). When the family became a sub-division of wider social divisions such as class, caste, territory, political allegiances or religions, the positive significance vanished. Marriages were contracted according to criteria which, though not always explicit, were based on wealth, power or profession. Sharing and reciprocity, the sometimes brutal authenticity of personal relationships, were blurred and conjugal unions became a means of furthering the interests of society, promiscuity being tolerated in so far as it was consistent with current economic and ideological motivations. Men knew which were the women they had to give up, but without knowing precisely to whom. Indeed giving was no longer compulsory, and neither, strictly speaking, was exogamy, since marriages were not contracted according to predetermined rules of kinship. Agamy had replaced exogamy and endogamy.

Owing to the mobility and growth of populations the biological consequences of incest are now practically non-existent. Moreover its practice cannot endanger a society based on property and state control. In primitive societies the family served as unit, model and motivation. Society depended on matrimonial alliances and these depended on society. The prohibition of incest referred to group relations, not to the relations between a man and a woman. Its transgression would jeopardize social and material stability, but could only marginally affect individual relationships. On the other hand if present day society perishes it will not be because incest is tolerated, the sexes have equal rights or adult males no longer lay down the law, but because trading will have become impossible through the development of private enterprise and because commerce, industry and the police force will be incapable of exchanging, producing and protecting profit and the state.

That universal law of laws, the prohibition of incest, is in fact no more than a restriction, one aspect of a group transaction, the negative of the relations between the sexes, and has no impact on positive social interactions. It is not inseparable from society and culture; rather, our specific society and culture have made it inevitable, but only in the domestic sphere where the bonds of affinity and security which unite small groups and close kin still survive. In other words it concerns interindividual rather than social relations.

The terms 'biological couple', 'biological individual' or 'amorphous sex life' are meaningless when applied to primitive or animal societies; they may have some significance when referring to large, organized societies, highly conscious of their level of evolution, with a definite split between the private and the public, the organic and the social, the individual and the community. And the prohibition of incest is taken so seriously precisely because it has been displaced from the public to the private world. It has become a symptom of divided sociability and serves merely to check the passions and to restrict the sphere of communication between the sexes.

The fact that the prohibition of incest is not universal has a considerable bearing on my whole theory. We will never be able to recreate the past nor even assess *a priori* the value of interpretations and evidence which might help us to understand it. But social and psychological events which are now taking place could well decide the matter in favour of my theory; only time can tell. However the significance of these events is unquestionable. The tensions between the sexes and between generations have reached a climax. These are usually only perceived in relation to the economy and to general social changes, but division, domination and non-communication, in fact everything which affects them, occur within the family circle. A social system in which the family is preserved cannot significantly modify intersex and intergeneration relations, even if it establishes civic and social equality. However urbanization, by reducing the family unit to father, mother and children, though this first increased parental authority (now undivided since there were no other adults in the household to share it), later diminished it legally when the education and social and industrial integration of children were transferred to (or at least shared by) the State. The difference between paternal and maternal domination has become negligible in consequence. But if it were proved that the prohibition of incest is really involved in the reproduction of sexual hierarchy then this prohibition would have to be abrogated as the first condition for any modification of the family institution or its replacement by a new kind of relationship based on reciprocity and sexual equality. This does not mean that incest should be indulged, but only that the prohibition would be lifted; it would no longer be a regulating principle in individual relationships or a negative dimension of social existence. Incest (like cannibalism, for instance) would not be considered as a possibility and would therefore no longer have to be restricted by law.

If, on the other hand, it turns out that society cannot survive without sexual inequality, that humanity cannot or will not do without it, or even that after equality has been achieved the prohibition still survives, then my theory will have been proved invalid. Until then even the most coherent logical construction is no more than speculation.

Primitive kinship societies are based on exogamic division and the prohibiton of incest. Neither institution seems to have preceded the other; they are mutually dependent and their origins, common or otherwise, are obscure. They have influenced a great many social systems in varying forms and combinations. Different communities always solve their problems in different ways and such solutions are never permanent, though remoteness may give a misleading impression of uniformity. However some of these solutions have resisted time better than others.

The hierarchy and discrimination based on sex and age which are to be found in primate societies were adopted and adapted by the first human societies. Cooperation, nomadism and the separation of hunting and gathering groups, with their distinctive skills and environments, placed these institutions in a different intellectual and organic context requiring a new definition of reality. The family, by including the male in the relationship between mother and children, and children in the relationship between male and female, ensured their permanent coexistence through a new collaboration of the sexes which served the purposes of production. Marriage, in one form or another, was the only union acknowledged and sanctioned by society.

Furthermore the diversity of activities compelled communities to spread over vaster, more varied territories. The network of interdependencies became more complex and required mutual obligations and privileges and a flexible structure allowing for alternating periods of isolation and communality. The distribution of individuals, supplies, implements and territories was based on an exogamic system of exchange. Society incorporated and socialized nomadism by creating this interdependence between its various clans and families. And since the original priority of males was not affected by such developments it gradually involved their specific activities.

This coherent complex consisting of human beings and the means, implements and skills they had acquired could only be maintained and transmitted through sexual reproduction. The union of a man and a woman in marriage and of male and female groups in society welded together two distinct fragments of the material universe – the animal and the vegetable worlds – and two separate spheres. Sexuality transcended its organic definition to involve nature, while nature involved sexuality to transcend its material definition. Division was now a necessity governing cosmic order and ensuring its permanence. But to maintain masculine priorities within the new division, or to allow male and female groups to follow their separate vocations without impairing masculine authority over the whole population, it was imperative that the women of the clan should be exchanged through marriage transactions for women from other clans who, as outsiders, were naturally subordinates.

The prohibition of incest established the separation of the sexes and forced the weaker to become a negotiable quantity for the stronger. At the same time it reflects the broader significance of their relations and constitutes the hierarchy proper to such relations. Obviously this reconstruction can always be challenged either by denying the status of society to animal communities, or by defining society as an exclusively human attribute. But what cannot be refuted is the fact that the evolutionary sequence progressed 'chemically', from primate to human social structures, and not 'alchemically' from a state of nature to a state of society. From the very beginning our species chose the harder way. Then, to compensate for the sometimes unforeseen difficulties it encountered, it decided that this choice was nothing less than a miracle.

[XII]

Retrospect

1 Change and Creation

(a) Historical nature

The idea that nature and society are mutually contradictory is one of the few established notions which, notwithstanding the lively sceptiscism of scientific thought, is still prevalent. Yet so long as man and society are set outside and against nature, and nature is seen as static and uniform and societies as unique and dynamic the problem of the relation of man and society to nature cannot be solved.

Nature is far from uniform or static, since each species constantly transforms substances and energies to suit its needs (man being no exception); a lack of such interventions and participations in the cycle of events in a specific environment would be highly unnatural and artificial. Man's contact with nature has never been direct; it has always been mediated through knowledge structures via his senses and his intellect. We have no other means of knowing the world around us.

Even nature reserves intended to protect nature from human intervention can only preserve something on which we have already left our mark. Africa was quite a different continent when man first emerged. The discovery of fire reduced the forested areas, increasing the pasturelands where herds thrived and proliferated. Pollution is not a novelty and it has produced many natural sites in its time. Even the distinction between wild and domestic animals is arbitrary if it is taken to mean that the former have not been influenced by man's presence on the planet. There is not a single species that has been able to avoid this influence. Some have become extinct, others have thrived, but all have had to modify their habits as a result of agriculture or hunting. Apart from such direct impact, man has frequently acted as a natural phenomenon producing biological transformations.[100] For example the macaque monkeys of Eastern Africa, who, when first observed in a deforested area, were assumed to be a non-arboreal variety similar to the African baboon, almost certainly conformed to the arboreal habits of their species until intensive cultivation and the deforestation of the whole region deprived them of their natural habitat and compelled them to live on the ground. At most it could be said that wild animals are those whole existence has adapted to the conditions created by man, while those involved in the circuit of his environmental interactions are domestic; but neither is uninfluenced by his presence.

Pollution began before the emergence of *Homo sapiens* and has never ceased. It does not threaten our natural, genetic constitution any more than predation, meat-eating, bipedalism or the changes in brain volume which produced language and thought. The concept of a world that has not been created in part by man is unrealistic; man must be included among the natural forces which have helped to shape his environment; otherwise, as Freud said, nature is 'an empty abstraction, devoid of practical interest'.[101] Nature is not uniform. We are dependent on our environment, for we have created it as much as it has created us. The discovery of new substances and new methods inevitably influences the general structure of the world and the course of history. The very emergence of life altered the composition of hydrocarbons by substituting biogenetic reactions for chemico-physical reactions. Organic and inorganic systems affect each other. First cellular division, and then sexual reproduction had a positive influence on organic evolution and created the environment we are now invited to protect after protecting ourselves against it for centuries. The components and the outline of the material world vary from one galaxy and from one era to another. The notion that nature is always and everywhere identical is refuted by the evidence of temporal and spatial variability. The idea of a 'return to nature' is meaningless.

Nature is a constellation of substances organized into simultaneous or sequential systems. Biological phenomena such as natural selection initiated an historical process. With the emergence of mankind sociality became increasingly forceful and distinctive and influenced the general development. The passage from primate to man was a gradual process that directed pre-existing aptitudes towards new ends, not a sudden departure from nature. The reproduction of the human race created an original type of beings and of collectivities and thus established a sequence of behaviour patterns, aptitudes and conventions distributed according to an objective law and corresponding to a system of environmental exchanges. As man's faculties and skills developed together with his physical and anatomical evolution, his perception and intelligence increased and contributed to the species' chances of reproduction and survival. The use of implements (among which social coordination may be included) further assisted its preservation.

The decisive factor in the emergence of man was not a chance mutation but the coincidence, at a favourable stage in genetic and social development of two factors: a number of individuals (the male bands) possessing a range of skills and aptitudes (upright stance, bipedal locomotion, use of artefacts); and extended exploitable food resources. When the species, instead of being preyed upon by other animals, became predatory, a whole range of incidental aptitudes, attitudes, implements and biological potentialities were generally adopted and the essentially vegetable environment was suddenly extended to include animal life. As a result, exploratory excursions covered wider territories, and this forest-dwelling species annexed the plains. Increasing specialization led to the estrangement of hunters from gatherers, and the whole animal world, including primates, figured henceforth as elements of the environment. Then, with the growing complexity of social organization, more and more independent of purely biological determination, a human species appeared.

This separation of hunters from gatherers was the evolutionary turning point where man and animal parted company. It promoted the numerical growth as well as the diversity of the species. Bipedalism gave rise to neuro-physiological changes which in turn led to new modes of communication and interaction. Language and symbolic thought then became part of our genetic heritage, contributing to the integration of attitudes and the distribution of information, and thus influencing individual and collective relations. The species was constitutionally adapted and transformed without an actual split having occurred at a determinable moment in time. What took place was a gradual development consistent with its natural constitution. Because of the natural division into distinct human groups involving different sections of the environment, different activities could be pursued within a single territory. This evolutionary eclecticism furthered practical and occupational selectivity so that certain activities became secondary, and were later abandoned in favour of others or integrated into the whole complex.

Man was the creature of this first division, not its creator. Other divisions followed, entailing further transformations and consequences. Each stage of development represents a natural, dynamic mutation of the original material structure. The earlier stages are no more 'natural' than their successors. Arts and skills mediate between what is human and what is not; they must be seen as prenatural rather than antinatural, as indispensable elements of the process which has produced the world which surrounds us. Paul Klee said of the artist that his art 'makes him aware — not of nature — but of the only thing that matters: creation as genesis',[102] and this could be said of man in general. Nature cannot exist without labour and understanding. Moreover the popular notion of an ever-expanding technology slowly and relentlessly encroaching upon and destroying our natural world is entirely misleading. The natural world is not being turned into a technological world; it is simply evolving.

(b) Negative and positive society

Seen as one among many societies each of which influenced the organisms
and environments involved, human society emerges as both manipulator of
nature and autonomous structure. On the one hand it is a positive material
force confronting other material forces, a group of men united in a
common endeavour to create an adequate environment; on the other it is
negative and introverted, possessing an evolutionary and historical
dynamism of its own.

Man's ability to maintain and reproduce his organic and intellectual
characteristics, to renew human and non-human resources is distinctly
positive As Tinbergen observes, it is essential for an understanding of
instinctual behaviour in general to realize that the different instincts are
not mutually independent.[103] They are motivated by specific activities
which define and condition their interactions and their impact. They
include tendencies motivated by thirst, hunger, aggressivity and
procreation as well as the epistemic instinct which, though less obvious
and less directly related to a particular neuro-physiological system,
nonetheless is a significant motivating power. Anthropoids, as we have
seen, are notoriously inquisitive, and a number of activities, such as
exploration and grooming, indirectly satisfy such a tendency. Cognition
and recognition dispel the monotony of existence and encourage
innovation and invention. Man shares this trait with a number of species,
and the nomadism of hunters, as well as the mobility of populations,
undoubtedly corresponds to this tendency. Society combines and exploits
these instincts which in turn influence the structure of the biosphere.
Material culture – technology, energy control, demography and so on[104]
– was not created spontaneously to satisfy human needs. It corresponds
to a tendency common to all living creatures to propagate and to
coordinate their existence within a suitable ecology. Society requires and
achieves a natural basis which is incessantly renewed, not because an
individual constructs an implement or makes an experiment, but because
material energy is translated into physical and intellectual attributes. Our
successes and our failures concern the whole of nature in so far as they
influence mutual adaptation.

Society's negative aspect is expressed in the sequence of interests,
activities and interactions centred around the power, wealth and hierarchy
which divide and coordinate classes, sexes and regions, enlisting energies
and promoting communication. Unity is maintained at the expense of
individuality, and solidarity at the expense of independence. Ceremonials,
rituals, rewards and punishments preserve the group spirit, justify
regulations and promote loyalty and self-effacement; they encourage
reciprocity while maintaining distinctions. Education and tradition
preserve the continuity of the structure and help to maintain the delicate
balance between a required diversity of interests and activities and an

adequate control of such diversified groups. Each individual must be conditioned to fit the specific function he has to fulfil in society, while conforming at all times to its conventions. Discipline, repression and inhibition are the means to such an end. However the continuity of a society, human or otherwise, depends on the biological individual whose organic, instinctive and intellectual existence must be ensured. He must not be deprived of all his original impulses and aptitudes, nor should these be entirely diverted from their original objects. If social intervention constricts individual existence this is because the methods employed are oppressive but not necessarily because they oppress any hidden, intrinsically free and spontaneously natural potential.

Our society is an institution which inhibits what it stimulates. It both tempers and excites aggressive, epistemic and sexual tendencies, increases or reduces the chances of satisfying them according to class distinctions, and invents prohibitions together with the means of transgressing them. Its sole purpose, to date, is self-preservation, and it opposes change by means of laws and regulations. It functions on the basic assumption that it is unique, has nothing to learn and cannot be improved. Hence its unambiguous dismissal of all that is foreign to it. Even its presumed artificiality, which might be considered a shortcoming, is taken, on the contrary, for a further sign of superiority, since it is an attribute of mankind. As for all other societies, they are nothing but the product of environmental and organic influences.

There is a tendency nowadays to contrast society and nature. Yet social structures cannot be isolated from the materials of which they are made. A society is an autonomous system included in a vaster cosmic system and its specific reality is part of the totality of natural and social orders. It is the collective energy and activity which involve performance, knowledge and resources, as well as the translation of these into wealth, power and ideology. Neither aspect is more important than the other.

2 Re-entering Nature

Societies are threatened organisms. They attempt the almost impossible task of conciliating law, convention and hierarchy with individual initiative — or of adapting social pressures to the requirements of a given population and historical moment. They must fulfil two basic functions: the general function, common to all species, of linking organisms and environment, and the specifically human function of ensuring the social distribution of wealth and power.

The popular notion that the general function causes tension and is redundant springs from various causes. Man has always been reluctant to admit that his social structure is only one among many such structures. He likes to see himself as different, independent of natural and biological influences. He thinks of his society as an efficient, active entity opposed to the passive material world which he exploits and subdues in order that, as Lévi-Strauss says: 'Henceforth, history would make itself by itself. Society, placed outside and above history, would be able to exhibit once again that regular and, as it were, crystalline structure which the best-preserved of primitive societies teach us is not antagonistic to the human condition.' [105]

We tend to think that if this general function persists, it can only be because we have not been able to do away with scarcity. Societies still depend on the environment and thus on their own exertions which unavoidably entail inequalities, but these will disappear as soon as the problem of scarcity has been solved. Scientific and technological progress will eliminate labour and man will be totally independent of nature: 'Obviously, men and events can only be seen, to date, in the context of scarcity,' says Sartre, 'that is in a society *as yet* [my italics] incapable of freeing itself from its needs and thus from nature, and which is therefore subservient to technology and tools.' [106] In a land of plenty man will be free from necessity and from nature.

But in fact society and nature are mutually dependent and their relationship is indestructible. Society cannot step out of history and settle permanently in a golden age; nor has it ever known a golden age and been banished from it. A break with the natural world is not the answer to our problems. Where then does the answer lie? Might it not be precisely in the relationship between the two functions of society?

The discrepancy between scientific and technological progress and the material advantages it has provided is generally ascribed to an over-shooting of prescribed aims. In fact, however, it results from a wilful neglect of society's general function. Because we refuse to see the relation between ecology, industry, science and demography, which are the various facets of a single process involving society and environment, we tend to consider this general function as sporadic and fragmented, though temporarily unavoidable. On the contrary, the natural function of society is an objective force involved with other cosmic forces; it is a permanent, not a transitory phenomenon which might enable us to resocialize nature rather than abandon it. Humanity may vanish from the face of the earth, and is quite capable of destroying itself, but until then its involvement with nature is part of the human condition within its historical and evolutionary context.

Man would master matter, purloin physical and biological energy and unravel cosmic mysteries when his own survival and that of the surrounding world really depend on his own organic, social and intellectual faculties. What is at stake is not the conquest of nature but the creation of man. Judaeo-Christianity asserts that God gave all the creatures of the earth into man's custody together with the earth itself.

Rationalist philosophy asserts that knowledge is power and that man's intellect has given him mastery over the world. Both suggest that man's relationship with the animate and inanimate world – or with other men – should be based on exploitation. Though it is hopelessly inadequate, this interpretation of the world as object and of man as its exploiter has produced positive results in the past. But today what is required is not to conquer nature but to make peace with it. As Engels said: 'At every step we are reminded that we by no means rule over nature like a conqueror over a foreign people, like someone standing outside nature – but that we, with flesh, blood and brain, belong to nature, and exist in its midst.' [107]

NOTES

Introduction

1 D. Hume, *Treatise on Human Nature,* (London 1758), II, p. 265.
2 H. Bergson, *The Two Sources of Morality and Religion,* trans. R. Ashley Audra and Clondesley Brereton (London 1935).
3 P. Bidney, *Theoretical Anthropology* (New York 1959), p. 18.
4 S. Moscovici, *Essai sur l'histoire humaine de la nature* (Paris 1968).
5 W. Shakespeare, *The Winter's Tale,* IV : 3, 90-2.
6 C. Lévi-Strauss, *The Elementary Structures of Kinship,* (London 1968).
7 A. Leroi-Gourhan, *Le Geste et la parole* (Paris 1964), p. 205.
8 A. Kroeber, *The Nature of Culture* (Chicago 1952).
9 C. Lévi-Strauss, *The Elementary Structures of Kinship* (London 1968) 2nd edn.

Part ONE

1 V. C. Wyne-Edwards, *Animal Dispersion in Relation to Social Behaviour* (New York 1962).
2 The following are the works to which I mainly refer in this section. The theories of Crook and Hall are those with which I am most in sympathy, though our terminology and interpretations may often be at variance.
S. A. Altmann, 'A Field Study of the Socio-biology of Rhesus Monkeys, *Macaca Mulatta', Annals of New York Academy of Science,* C II: 2, (1962) pp. 238-435.
C. R. Carpenter (ed.) *Naturalistic Behaviour of Nonhuman Primates* (Philadelphia 1964).
M. R. A. Chance, 'Social Structure of a Colony of *Macaca Mulatta', British Journal of Animal Behaviour,* IV (1956), pp. 1-13.
J. H. Crook, 'Evolutionary Change in Primate Societies', *Science Journal,* III: 6 (1967), pp. 66-72.
J. H. Crook (ed.) *Social Behaviour in Birds and Mammals* (London/New York 1970).
J. H. Crook and P. Aldrich-Black, 'Ecological and Behavioural Contrasts Between Sympatic Ground-Dwelling Primates in Ethiopia', *Folia Primatologica,* VIII (1968), pp. 192-227.

J. H. Crook and J. S. Gartlan, 'Evolution of Primate Societies', *Nature,* CCX (1966), pp. 1200-1203.

I. De Vore (ed.), *Primate Behaviour: Field Studies of Monkeys and Apes* (New York 1965).

T. Dobzhansky, 'Cultural Direction of Human Evolution'. *Human Biology,* XXXV (1963), pp. 311-16.

J. S. Gartlan 'Structure and Function in Primate Society', *Folia Primatologica,* VIII (1968), pp. 89-120.

K. R. L. Hall, various articles in De Vore, *Primate Behaviour* and Jay, *Primates.*

P. Jay (ed.), *Primates: Studies in Adaptation and Variability* (New York 1968).

H. Kummer, 'Social Organisation of Hamadryas Baboons', *Bibliotheca Primatologica,* VI (1968), pp. 1-189.

H, Kummer, 'Two Variations in the Social Organisation of Baboons', in Jay, *Primates.*

H, Kummer and F. Kurt, 'Social Units of a Free-Living Population of Hamadryas Baboons', *Filoa Primatologica,* I (1963), pp. 4-19.

W. A. Mason, 'Sociability and Social Organisation in Monkeys and Apes', *Advances in Experimental Social Psychology,* I (1964), pp. 277-305.

J. J. Petter, 'Recherches sur l'écologie et l'éthologie des Lemuriens malgaches', *Mémoires du Musée National d'Histoire Naturelle,* Série A XXVII (1962), pp. 1-46.

T. E. Rowell, 'Variability in the Social Organisation of Primates', in D. Morris (ed.), *Primate Ethology,* (London 1967).

From the following I have drawn a great deal of useful information:

M. R. A. Chance, 'Attention Structure as the Basis of Primate Rank Order', *Man,* II (1967) pp. 503–18.

W. Etkin, 'Social Behavioural Facts in the Emergence of Man', *Human Biology,* LXV (1963), pp. 299–310.

R. A. Hinde and Y. Spencer-Booth, 'The behaviour of Socially Living Rhesus Monkeys in Their First Two and a Half Years', *Animal Behaviour,* XV (1967), pp. 169–96.

K. Imanishi, 'Social Organisation of Subhuman Primates in their Natural Habitat', *Current Anthropology,* I (1960), pp. 393, 407.

J. Itani, 'Paternal Care in the Wild Japanese Monkey, *Macaca Fuscata',* *Primates,* II (1957), pp. 61-93.

G. B. Koford, 'Rank of Mothers and Sons in Bands of Rhesus Monkeys', *Science,* CXLI (1963), pp. 356–7.

G. D. Mitchell, 'Paternalistic Behaviour in Primates', *Psychological Bulletin,* VII (1969), pp. 399–417.

V. Reynolds, 'Kinship and the Family in Monkeys, Apes and Man', *Man,* III (1968), pp. 209–23.

V. Reynolds, 'Open Groups in Hominid Evolution', *Man,* I (1966), pp. 441–52.

T. E. Rowell, 'Hierarchy in the Organisation of a Captive Baboon Group', *Animal behaviour,* XIV (1966), pp. 420–43.

D. S. Sade, 'Some Aspects of Parent-Offspring and Sibling Relations in a

Group of Rhesus Monkeys, with a Discussion of Grooming', *American Journal of Physical Anthropology*, XXIII (1965), pp. 1–18.
Vandenbergh, 'The Development of Social Structure in Free-Ranging Monkeys', *Behaviour*, XXIX (1967), pp. 179–95.
4 M. Chance and C. Jolly, *Social Groups of Monkeys, Apes and Men* (London 1970).
5 J. Itani, 'Paternal Care in the Wild Japanese Monkey, *Macaca Fuscata'*, *Journal of Primatology*, II (1962), p. 86.
6 G. Bataille, *L'érotisme* (Paris 1957), p. 236.

Part TWO

1 The following have been very useful in helping me to clarify my ideas:
L. R. and S. R. Binford, 'A Preliminary Analysis of Functional Variability in the Mousterian of Levallois Facies', *American Anthropologist*, LXVIII (1966), pp. 239–94.
M. Detienne and J.-P. Vernant, 'La métis du renard et du poulpe', *Revue d'études grecques*, LXXXII (1969), pp. 291–317.
K. R. L. Hall, 'Tool-using Performances as Indicators of Behavioural Adaptability', *Current Anthropology*, IV (1963), pp. 479–94.
K. J. and C. Hayes, 'The Cultural Capacity of Chimpanzees', *Human Biology*, XXVI (1954), pp. 288–303.
G. H. Hewes, 'Hominid Bipedalism: Independent Evidence for the Food-Carrying Theory', *Science*, CXLVI (1964), pp. 416–18.
H. J. Jerison, 'Interpreting the Evolution of the Brain', *Human Biology*, XXXV (1963), pp. 263–91.
R. B. Lee and I. De Vore, Man the Hunter (Chicago 1968).
A. Leroi-Gourhan, *Le geste et la parole*.
P. R. Marler, 'Animal Communication Signals; Function and Structure', *Science*, CLVII (1967), pp. 769–74.
J. Napier, 'The Evolution of the Hand', *Scientific American*, CCVII (1962), p. 157.
K. P. Oakley, *Man the Toolmaker* (London 1961).
T. A. Sebeok (ed.), *Animal Communication* (Bloomington 1968).
C. H. Southwick, *Primate Social Behaviour* (Princeton 1963).
I. Vine, 'Communication by Facial Visual Signals', in Crook, *Social Behaviour*, pp. 279–354.
S. L. Washburn, 'Australopithecines: The Hunters or the Hunted', *American Anthropologist*, LIX (1957), pp. 612–14.
S. L. Washburn, *Classification and Human Evolution* (London 1964).
S. L. Washburn, 'Speculations on the Interrelations of the History of Tools and Biological Evolution', *Human Biology*, XXXI (1959), pp. 21–31.
S. L. Washburn and C. S. Lancaster, 'The Evolution of Hunting' in N. Korn and F. Thomson (eds.), *Human Evolution* (New York 1973), p. 212.
S. Zuckerman, *The Social Life of Monkeys and Apes* (London 1932).
2 J. N. Spuhler, *The Evolution of Man's Capacity for Culture* (Detroit 1959), p.1.
3 A. Montagu, *The Human Revolution* (Clevelend 1965), p. 41.

4 C. L. Isaac, in Lee and De Vore, *Man the Hunter*, pp. 253–4.

5 Though a few scientists, of whom De Vore is one, appear to have adopted this attitude, they are still under the influence of Darwinian theories and anthropological models. Such work restricts itself to a descriptive level and lacks theoretical depth.

6 J. Helm, 'The Ecological Approach in Anthropology', *American Journal of Sociology*, LXVII (1962), pp. 630–9.
A. I. Hallowell, 'The Size of Algonkian Hunting Territories, a Function of Ecological Adjustment', *American Anthropologist*, LI (1949), pp. 35–45.
G. Bartholomew and J. Birdsell, 'Ecology and the Protohominids', *American Anthropologist*, LV (1953), pp. 481–98.

7 J. H. Crook, 'Cooperation in Primates', *The Eugenics Review*, LVIII (1966), p. 68.

8 S. L. Washburn, 'Australopithecines, The Hunters or the Hunted', in *American Anthropologist*, loc. cit.

9 A. Comfort, *The Nature of Human Nature* (New York 1968), p. 68.

10 L. R. and S. R. Binford, 'The Predatory Revolution', *American Anthropologist*, LXVIII (1966), pp. 508–12.

11 S. L. Washburn and C. S. Lancaster, 'The Evolution of Hunting' in Korn and Thomson, *Human Evolution*, p. 212.

12 K. P. Oakley, *Man the Tool-Maker*, p. 1.

13 V. G. Childe, *Social Evolution* (London 1951).

14 K. P. Oakley 'On Man's Fire, with Comments on Tool-Making and Hunting', in Washburn, *Social Life of Early Man* (Chicago 1961), p. 187.

15 W. S. Laughlin, 'Acquisition of Anatomical Knowledge by Ancient Man' in Washburn, *Social Life of Early Man*, p. 151.

16 S. L. Washburn and F. C. Howell, 'Human Evolution and Culture', in Sol Tax (ed.) *Evolution after Darwin* (Chicago 1960), I, p. 49.

17 E. Mayer, 'Taxonomic Categories in Fossil Hominids', *Quarterly Biology*, XV (1950), pp. 109–18.

18 J. Monod, *Chance and Necessity*, trans. Ansryn Wainhouse (London 1972).

19 *Ibid.*

20 C. Elton, *The Ecology of Animals* (London 1968), p. 61.

21 D. H. Scott, 'Cultural and Natural Checks on Population Growth', in A. P. Vayda, *Environment and Cultural Behaviour* (New York 1969), p. 191.

22 E. Boserup, *Evolution agraire et pression démographique* (Paris 1970).

23 K. Marx, *Grundrisse* (London 1973), p. 605.

24 S. Moscovici, 'Le marxisme et la question naturelle', *L'Homme et la Société*, (Paris 1968), pp. 59–109.

25 S. L. Washburn and C. S. Lancaster in Lee and De Vore, *Man the Hunter*, p. 293.

26 S. Moscovici, *Essai sur l'histoire humaine de la nature*.

27 E. W. Caspari, 'Some Genetic Implications of Human Evolution', in S. L. Washburn, *Social Life of Early Man*, op. cit. p. 274.

28 T. Dobzhansky, 'The Present Evolution of Man', *Scientific American* (September 1960), p. 207.

Part *THREE*

1 Euripides, *Andromache.* The Loëb Classical Library (London 1912), pp. 174–176.
2 B. Milinowski, *Crime and Custom in Savage Society* (London 1926), p. 64.
3 C. Lévi-Strauss, *The Elementary Structures of Kinship* (London 1968).
4 G. Charbonnier, *Conversations with Claude Lévi-Strauss,* trans. J. & D. Weightman (London 1970), pp. 147–8.
5 K. Lorenz, *Studies in Animal and Human Behaviour* (London 1970).
6 *Ibid.*
7 H. Callan, *Ethology and Society* (Oxford 1970).
8 S. Freud, *Totem and Taboo,* standard edn., XIII (London 1968).
9 F. R. Service, *Primitive Social Organisation* (New York 1968), p. 69.
10 S. L. Washburn and P. C. Jay, *Perspectives on Human Evolution* (New York 1968).
11 A. Leroi-Gourhan, *Le geste et la parole.*
12 V. Reynolds, 'Kinship and the Family in Monkeys, Apes and Man', in *Man,* loc. cit.
13 J. D. Clark, *The Prehistory of Southern Africa* (London 1959), p. 39.
14 M. Mauss, 'Essai sur les variations saisonnières des sociétés eskimos', *Année sociologique,* IX (1905), p. 65.
15 C. D. Forde, *Habitat, Economy and Society* (New York 1963).
16 J. H. Steward, 'Theory of Cultural Change', *Urbana,* III.
17 H. Watanabe, 'Subsistence and Ecology of Northern Food Gatherers with Special Reference to the Ainu', in Lee and De Vore, *Man the Hunter,* p. 75.
18 L. de Heusch, *Pourgoui l'épouser?* (Paris 1971), p. 105.
19 J. H. Steward, 'Causal Factors and Process in the Evolution of Pre-Farming Societies', in Lee and De Vore, *Man the Hunter,* pp. 330–1.
20 C. Lévi-Strauss, 'The Family' in H. L. Shapiro (ed.) *Man, Culture and Society* (New York 1956), p. 269.
21 C. Lévi-Strauss, *The Elementary Structures of Kinship* (London 1968).
22 J. B. Birdsell, 'On Population Structure in Generalized Hunting and Collecting Societies', *Evolution,* XII (1958), pp. 189–95.
23 M. Mauss, *Sociologie et anthropologie,* Paris 1965, p. 161.
24 E. E. Evans-Pritchard, *Social Anthropology* (New York 1962).
25 G. Roheim, *Héros phalliques et symboles maternels dans la mythologie australienne* (Paris 1970).
26 M. Mauss, *Sociologie et anthropologie,* p. 194.
27 C. Lévi-Strauss, *Les structures élémentaires de la parenté,* p. 55.
28 Ibid., p. 64.
29 Ibid., p. 616.
30 B. Malinowski, *La vie sexuelle des sauvages du nord-ouest de la Mélanésie* (Paris 1930), p. 51.
31 C. Lévi-Strauss, *The Elementary Structures of Kinship* (London 1968).
32 Ibid.
33 Ibid.
34 Ibid.

35 J. Frazer, Totemism and Exogamy (London 1910),IV p. 97.
36 R. Jaulin, *La Paix blanche* (Paris 1970), p. 296.
37 L. W. Simmons, *The Role of the Aged in Primitive Societies*, s.1. 1970.
38 D. F. Aberle *et al.*, 'The Incest Taboo and the Mating Patterns of Animals', American Anthropologist, LXV (1963), pp. 253–65.
39 G. Bateson, *La cérémonie du naven* (Paris 1971).
40 M. Mead, *Sex and Temperament in Three Primitive Societies* (New York 1953).
41 A. F. Radcliffe-Brown and D. Forde, *African Systems of Kinship and Marriage* (New York 1950).
42 L. de Heusch, *Essais sur le symbolisme de l'inceste royal en Afrique* (Brussels 1958).
43 B. Malinowski, *La vie sexuelle*, pp. 490, 497.
44 S. Freud, *Totem and Taboo*, p. 5.
45 Ibid., p. 121.
46 Aristotle, *Politics*, Harmondsworth 1962) I:IV.
47 C. Lévi-Strauss, *From Honey to Ashes*, trans. J. and D. Weightman (London 1973) pp. 285–6.
48 K. L. Little, 'The Role of Secret Society in Cultural Specialisation', *American Anthropologist*, LI (1949), pp. 199–212.
49 R. Lowie, *Traité de sociologie primitive* (Paris 1969), p. 248.
50 Ibid., p. 92.
51 G. Bateson, *La cérémonie du naven*, p. 211.
52 G. Roheim, 'Psychoanalysis of Primitive Cultural Types', *International Journal of Psychoanalysis*, XVIII (1932), p. 152.
53 E. Durkheim, 'La Prohibition de l'inceste et ses origines', *Année sociologique*, I (1896), p. 40.
54 M. Douglas, *Natural Symbols* (London 1970).
55 F. W. Young and A. A. Bucdayan, 'Menstrual Taboos and Social Rigidity', *Ethnology*, IV (1965), pp. 225–40.
56 A. Strathern, 'The Female and Male Spirit Cults in Mount Hajen', *Man*, V (1970), pp. 571–86.
57 E. Durkheim, 'La Prohibition de l'inceste et ses origines', *Année sociologique*, I (1896), p. 68.
58 R. Jaulin, *La Mort Sara* (Paris 1971).
59 Ibid., p. 124.
60 E. Norbeck, D. E. Walker and M. Cohen, 'The Interpretation of Data: Puberty Rites', *American Anthropologist*, LXIV (1962), pp. 463–85.
61 G. Bateson, *La cérémonie du naven*, p. 132.
62 N. N. Tindale in Roheim, *Héros phaliques*, p. 215.
63 G. Roheim, *Héros phaliques*, p. 215.
64 M. Douglas, *Natural Symbols*, p. 133.
65 R. le Vine, 'Sex Roles and Economic Change in Africa', *Ethnology*, V (1966), p. 191.
66 C. Lévi-Strauss, 'The Family' in Shapiro, *Man, Culture and Society*, p. 275.
67 M. Mauss, *Essais de sociologie* (Paris 1968 and 1969), p. 137.
68 R. Fox, *Kinship and Marriage*, (Baltimore 1967), p. 32.
69 M. Mead, *Male and Female* (New York 1949), p. 164.

70   G. P. Murdock, *Social Structure* (New York 1949), p. 7.

71   E. Durkheim, *De la division du travail social*, 7th edn. (Paris 1960), p. 24.

72   D. A. F. de Sade, *Justine ou les malheurs de la vertu*, S.1., 1969, p. 216.

73   J. H. Steward, *chapter cit.*, p. 335.

74   S. Moscovici, *Essai sur l'histoire humaine de la nature.*

75   G. Calame-Griaule and Z. Ligers, 'L'homme-hyène dans les traditions soudanaises', *L'Homme*, I (1961), pp. 89–119.

76   F. Engels, 'The Origin of Family, Private Property and the State' in *Marx Engels Selected Works* II (Moscow 1964).

77   L. Tiger, *Men in Groups* (London 1969).

78   B. Malinowski, *The Family among the Australian Aborigines; a Sociological Study* (London 1913), p. 287.

79   C. Lévi-Strauss, *The Savage Mind*, London 1962.

80   C. Lévi-Strauss, *Introduction to a Science of Mythology*, trans. J. & D. Weightman, 4 volumes.

81   E. Evans-Pritchard, *La Femme dans les sociétés primitives* (Paris 1971), p. 41.

82   F. W. Young, 'The Function of Male Initiation Ceremonies', *American Journal of Sociology*, LXVIII (1962), p. 381.

83   T. Hobbes, *De Civitate*, ch. IX.

84   G. Roheim, *Héros phaliques*, p. 108.

85   Lee and De Vore, *Man the Hunter*, p. 94.

86   J. B. Birdsell, 'On Population Structure' in *Evolution*, p. 196.

87   G. Davy, *La Foi jurée* (Paris 1922), p. 118.

88   G. Bataille, *L'érotisme*, p. 220.

89   S. Freud, *Totem and Taboo*, p. 125.

90   R. Firth, *We, the Tikopia, A Sociological Study of Kinship in Primitive Polynesia* (London 1936).

91   G. Lienhardt, *Social Anthropology* (London 1966).

92   Sophocles, *King Oedipus*, trans. E. F. Watling (Harmondsworth 1958) p. 61.

93   Sophocles, *Oedipus at Colonus*, trans. E. F. Watling (Harmondsworth 1958) p. 81.

94   Sophocles, *Antigone*, trans. E. F. Watling (Harmondsworth 1958) p. 144.

95   Ibid., p. 128.

96   Ibid., p. 141.

97   Ibid., p. 146.

98   Ibid., p. 140.

99   C. Lévi-Strauss, *The Origin of Table Manners.*

100 M. Chance and C. Jolly, *Social Groups of Monkeys, Apes and Men.*

101 S. Freud, *The Future of an Illusion*, standard edn., XXI (London 1968), p. 56.

102 P. Klee, *Théorie de l'art moderne* (Paris 1964), p. 28.

103 N. Tinbergen, *The Study of Instinct* (Oxford 1969).

104 L. A. White, 'Energy and the Evolution of Culture', *American Anthropologist*, XLV (1943), pp. 335–56.

105 C. Lévi-Strauss, *The Scope of Anthropology* (London 1967), p. 49.

106 J.-P. Sartre, *Critique de la raison dialectique* (Paris 1960), p. 202.

107 F. Engels, *Dialectics of Nature* (Moscow 1964), p. 183.

Society Against Nature

EUROPEAN PHILOSOPHY AND THE HUMAN SCIENCES
General Editor: John Mepham

This is a new series of translations of important and influential works of
European thought in the fields of philosophy and the human sciences.

The scope of Moscovici's discussion is remarkable. He examines the discoveries and theories of the many sciences that can contribute to our understanding of the origin of man and of his social and cultural life. He discusses the attempts made by the physical anthropologists to reconstruct the evolutionary history of the hominids on the basis of studies of fossil remains. He examines the exciting results of studies of animals societies, in particular of primate societies. The work of Engels, Freud and Lévi-Strauss are subjected to searching criticism. Moscovici makes an important contribution here to that questioning of the family and of the repressive relationship between men and women that has been initiated by the women's movement.